ART SCHOOL

WATERCOLOURS

Step-by-step teaching through inspirational projects

HAZEL HARRISON

LORENZ BOOKS
LONDON • NEW YORK • SYDNEY • BATH

This paperback edition published in 1997 by Lorenz Books
an imprint of Anness Publishing Limited
Hermes House
88-89 Blackfriars Road
London SE1 8HA

© Anness Publishing Limited 1996

ISBN 1 85967 560 3

A CIP catalogue record for this book is available from the British Library

Publisher: Joanna Lorenz
Project Editor: Samantha Gray
Designer: Michael Morey
Photographers: Paul Forrester and John Freeman

Previously published as part of a larger compendium,
How to Paint and Draw

Printed and bound in Hong Kong

1 3 5 7 9 10 8 6 4 2

CONTENTS

ABOUT WATERCOLOUR

Since the 19th century, watercolour has been without question the most popular medium among amateur painters, and it continues to hold its position of pre-eminence today. It is not hard to find reasons for this. The rise of the medium coincided with the Victorian love of scenery and the natural world. Landscape and flowers were, and still are, the most frequently painted subjects, and water-colour, with its fluidity, freshness and sparkle, is perfect for both.

It is far from being a medium solely for amateurs. More and more professional artists are turning to watercolour, and their subject matter is less limited. The medium is used for portraits and figure studies, for still lifes and cityscapes – indeed anything which can be painted is painted in watercolour.

WATERCOLOUR IN THE PAST

In fact, there is nothing new about the medium's popularity with professionals. Although we see mainly oil paintings when we visit historic collections of paintings, giving the impression that watercolour was regarded as a poor relation, this was dictated more by market forces than by anything else. On the whole, patrons and

OLIVIA FRASER
VICEROY'S HOUSE, NEW DELHI
(Above) *This striking painting, with its deep, rich colours, quickly dispels one of the common myths about watercolour – that it is a wishy-washy medium. The artist has controlled the paint with great assurance, taking the dark colour of the sky carefully around the edges of the building, and, on the building itself, laying one wash over another to create a patchwork of crisp-edged shapes.*

(Left) *Most watercolour artists own a selection of watercolour tubes and pans.*

JOHN LIDZEY
STILL LIFE WITH CANDLES

(Above) *This artist enjoys the unpredictability of watercolour; he encourages colours to bleed into one another, forming pools and backruns. However, although this still life appears free and spontaneous both in arrangement and in the manner of execution, the artist has chosen and placed the objects to form a pleasing composition, and he controls the watercolour with equal care, using pieces of cotton wool (cotton balls) to halt the flow of colours and to lift out soft highlights such as those on the candle flames and glass.*

RONALD JESTY
KIPPERS

(Right) *Although this painting and John Lidzey's are both still lifes, they could not be more different in approach and technique. Here there are no pools or runs of paint, and each edge is meticulously clean and clear. Jesty likes to try out unusual viewpoints in his still-life paintings, and here he has chosen to look down on the subject so that he can exploit the pattern made by the fish and the dark triangles.*

ELISABETH HARDEN
BLUE INTERIOR
(Above) *Painting interiors is a branch of still-life painting, although the subject is wider – you are dealing not just with objects but with their relationship to the surrounding space, so the perspective must be correct and the composition well-planned. The artist begins with rough sketches to plan the composition, then makes a careful drawing.*

RONALD JESTY
ROCK POOL
(Above) *This artist achieves his crisp effects and dense, glowing colours by working wet on dry, reserving highlights by painting carefully around them. You can see this effect on the background hills, the dark areas of rock and the water, where small patches of light-coloured paint have been left uncovered by later dark washes of colour.*

buyers wanted large, imposing oil paintings, particularly for commissioned portraits, so artists tended to reserve watercolour for their more private works, or for sketches used as reference for oil paintings.

A notable exception to this general rule was a group of 18th-century English painters who worked entirely in water-colour, painting landscapes and seascapes. Most particularly, the work of John Sell Cotman and Thomas Girtin (a genius who died tragically young) is well worth looking at in books of reproductions, as are the watercolours of J.M.W. Turner, whose unconventional and innovative techniques

KEN PAINE
AMELIA

(Below) *At first sight, this expressive portrait might well be mistaken for an oil painting, but in fact it is watercolour with the addition of Chinese white. The artist made no initial pencil drawing, but started immediately with a brush and thin paint, gradually increasing the amount of white.*

JOAN ELLIOTT BATES
FROM THE MULE PATH, SOUTH SPAIN

(Above) *Opaque paint has also been used for this charming landscape painted on location, but in this case it is gouache rather than watercolour mixed with white. The effect is very similar if the gouache is used fairly thinly, as it has been here, although you can achieve thicker, more solid colour if required.*

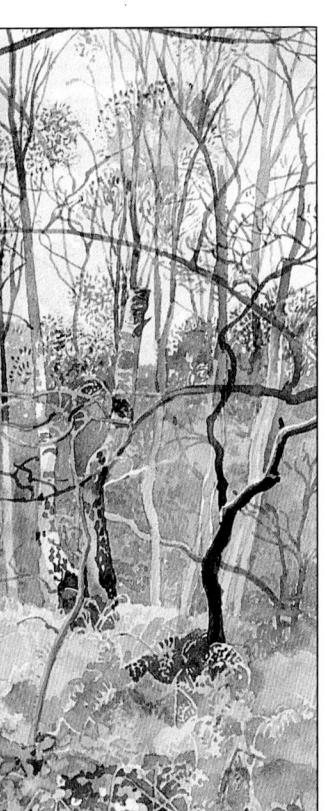

JULIETTE PALMER
BIRCH TRUNKS

(Left) *In this evocative and intricately detailed painting there is a strong emphasis on the pattern formed by the intertwining trunks and branches. The textures too have been described with great care, with a succession of small, delicate brushstrokes used for the trunks and distant clumps of twigs. The fine highlights in the foreground, which play an important part in the composition, were reserved by painting darker washes around lighter colours.*

are an endless source of inspiration. The giant of watercolour painting in America, at a slightly later date, was Winslow Homer, whose magical landscapes are now accorded the recognition they deserve (in his own lifetime, his oil paintings were better-known).

MYTHS AND PREJUDICES

For some reason, watercolour has attracted a more comprehensive – and often inexplicable – list of dos and don'ts than any other medium. People feel that there is a "correct" way of working and that any departure from this constitutes a kind of unfaithfulness to the medium. For example, we are told that we must never use opaque white because it will spoil the lovely translucence of the colours; while good painting aids such as masking fluid are

TREVOR CHAMBERLAIN
STILL-LIFE SESSION AT THE SEED WAREHOUSE

(Above) *Figure groups are not the easiest of subjects to tackle in watercolour, as it is not possible to make extensive corrections, but this painting shows that in skilled hands there is nothing the medium cannot do. Each brushstroke has been placed with care and, although the artist has worked largely wet into wet, he has controlled the paint so that it has not spread randomly over the surface.*

ELISABETH HARDEN
MAKING MARMALADE

Here the contrast between warm and cool colours has been skilfully exploited to highlight the dominant colour – orange. Although the colour scheme is deliberately limited, the artist has introduced a range of greens, blues and warm yellow-browns into the shadows to create variety and form colour links which unify the composition.

KAREN RANEY
ST-LAURENT-DE-CERDANS
(Left) *Watercolours are usually painted with the board held flat or at a slight angle, but in this on-the-spot painting the artist has worked with the board upright on an easel, causing the paint to run down the paper at the bottom of the picture. She has left the foreground otherwise undefined – the runs of paint hint at reflections in water.*

MIKE BERNARD
COW PARSLEY AND HOUSE
(Below) *Bernard seldom uses one medium on its own; here he has combined watercolour with expressive pen drawing. This has allowed him to introduce touches of detail into the foreground while keeping both the drawing and the watercolour washes unrestrained. The heads of the cow parsley are ink blots dropped from the pen, which have spread in places into the surrounding colours, and the linear highlights were achieved by scratching into dry paint.*

described as "mechanical" and therefore in some way immoral. Eyebrows are raised if you try anything new – it is simply not done. Interestingly, all these theories of correct procedure have only sprung up in this century, while the more rigid rules surrounding oil painting were the product of 18th- and 19th-century academic tradition and have since been largely abandoned. The best 19th-century watercolours, particularly those by Turner, reveal an enormous variety in the methods used, as well as many practices which might be frowned upon today. Turner used opaque paint; he moved the paint around on the picture surface and allowed colours to run; he smudged paint with his fingers and even scratched into it in places. In short, he used the medium as the servant of his ideas rather than the other way around.

The other myth about watercolour is that it is a particularly difficult medium to use. It is true that once you have made a mistake it isn't always possible to put it right, plus, of course, it can be hard to paint in the way that someone else thinks you should. Producing a good painting is never easy, whatever medium you use, but, once you have found your own way of working, the difficulties will be minimized.

PAINTS & BRUSHES

One of the many delights of watercolour is that initially you don't need a great deal in the way of materials: a small paintbox of colours, a few brushes, some paper and a jar for water, and you can make a start. The materials and equipment listed here are the basics; as you become more experienced and develop your own style and way of working, you may want to try out special brushes or a particular kind of palette, therefore it is best to start simply and build up as you go along.

THE PAINTS

Watercolours are produced in tubes, pans and half-pans; the only rather hard decision to make if you are starting from scratch is which to buy. Both have their advantages and disadvantages. Tube colours enable you to make strong, bright colours and to mix up a lot of paint quickly (ideal for those who work on a large scale). However, they are slightly tiresome for outdoor sketching as, unlike pans, they don't fit neatly into a paintbox. Pans are perhaps the most popular choice. They control the paint neatly so that colours don't run into one another, but it is more difficult to release the paint; indeed, you may have to scrub with your brush for some time to produce enough colour for a large wash.

Whichever type you decide on, do make sure that you buy the best-quality paints, known as "artist's" colours. Most manufacturers produce inexpensive ranges, sometimes called "student's" colours and sometimes given a name coined by the particular manufacturer. These usually contain a smaller proportion of pigment than artist's colours and are bulked out with fillers, sometimes making it impossible to achieve any depth of colour or to avoid patchiness, particularly over large areas.

WATERCOLOUR PALETTE

WATERCOLOUR PANS

WATERCOLOUR BOX

WATERCOLOUR TUBES

PAINTBOXES AND PALETTES

The kind of paintbox or palette you choose will depend on whether you are using pans (or half-pans) or tubes. For pans, you need a paintbox specially made for holding them in place, either with divisions for each pan or one long slot in which they all sit side by side. If you opt for tubes you must buy a separate palette or several small ones – or use an improvised palette such as an old plate. At one time you could buy metal paintboxes with small compartments into which the paint was squeezed; these have largely disappeared now, though you might still be lucky enough to find one.

BRUSHES

The best brushes for watercolour work are undoubtedly sables, but they are not recommended as part of a "starter kit" because they are prohibitively expensive, at least in the larger sizes. There are now many synthetic brushes, as well as sable and synthetic mixtures; brushes made from other soft hair such as ox and squirrel are also available. You may find you want to invest in one or two sables later on; if so, take heart from the fact that they are almost literally an investment – they will last a lifetime if you look after them.

Brushes are made in two basic shapes: round and flat. The former are essential, and you will probably require three different sizes: a small one for detail and two larger ones – the size will depend on the scale on which you work. Large flat brushes are useful for laying washes, but you won't need more than one to start with. There are other types of brush, such as mop brushes, which are also good for washes, but like sables these are expensive and should be regarded as a luxury item. You may want to invest in them later on.

COTTON BUDS

SELECTION OF WATERCOLOUR BRUSHES

WATERCOLOUR SPONGES

OTHER ITEMS

Most watercolour painters have a small natural sponge in their box of equipment, which can be used for "lifting out" paint and for mopping up paint that threatens to run. It is also a good alternative to brushes for laying washes. Of course, you also need a jar to hold water, and paper.

FLAT WATERCOLOUR BRUSH

PAPER

Watercolours are nearly always done on white paper; you can work on coloured paper, but this is the exception rather than the rule. The luminous quality that attracts so many people to watercolour work is the result of the white paper reflecting back through the layers of transparent paint. Colours are made lighter by using the paper as the white – heavily diluted paint allows much of the paper to show through, while thicker paint covers it.

PAPER SURFACES AND WEIGHTS

Basically there are three types of watercolour paper: rough, medium rough and smooth. They are all machine-made and are given names derived from the method of production. Rough paper has no alternative name, but smooth paper is known as "hot-pressed" and medium paper as "Not" (i.e. not hot-pressed), or sometimes as "cold-pressed". There are also handmade papers, which vary widely in texture. These are expensive and not always easy to handle; they are best left until you have gained a considerable degree of skill.

The vast majority of watercolour painters, amateur and professional alike, use Not surface paper. This has a slight texture, which holds the paint in place but does not break up the colour. Rough paper can be hard to manage, as the heavy texture tends to interfere with detail, and smooth paper can produce blotchy effects because the paint slides about on it.

All these papers are made in different weights, expressed as pounds (lb). This refers to the weight of a ream of paper – 500 sheets. Weights vary between 70lb, which is very thin, and 300lb, which is so thick that it resembles board. The thicker the paper the more it costs, but very thin paper must be stretched first.

STRETCHING WATERCOLOUR PAPER

Stretching the paper before use prevents it from buckling when you put on the wet paint. Colours laid over ridges and bumps may take a long time to dry out – and sometimes never do so, thus spoiling the effect of your finished work. Paper which is lighter than about 200lb usually needs to be stretched, particularly if you use a lot of wet washes or work wet into wet. The paper used for most types of watercolour sketching pads is 140lb, which will certainly buckle if you work on a large scale and build up many layers of colour, but it is reasonably safe for small-scale outdoor work.

1 ROUGH   2 WHITE

(3

1 *Soak the paper for a few minutes in a bath or sink. When you are sure it has absorbed the water evenly, lift it out by one corner, shake off the excess moisture and place it on the drawing board.*

2 *Cut four pieces of gumstrip, one for each side, and dampen well by running them across a wet sponge. The gumstrip should be 2.5 cm (1 in) wide for an average-sized painting and up to 5 cm (2 in) wide for a larger one.*

3 *Place a piece of gumstrip along one long edge of the paper and smooth it out firmly from the centre, to ensure that it makes contact with both paper and board at every point.*

4 *Repeat the process for the second long edge and then each alternate short edge. Don't worry if the paper begins to buckle slightly; it will dry flat.*

WHITE NOT   4 HOT-PRESSED   5, 6, 7 AND 8 TINTED NOT
(90LB)

GUMSTRIP

ADVICE ON MIXING

The first and perhaps the most difficult skill to master in any painting medium is mixing colours. Not only do you need to analyse the colours you see, you must also learn to think of them in terms of paint colours. It is easy to say that a sky is blue or that grass is green, but which blue and green would you choose from your paintbox? Which other colours could you mix in to achieve the effect you can see in your subject?

Most of this comes with experience and, it has to be said, after a certain amount of trial and error. But it is useful to know some facts about the paint colours themselves in order to understand what may or may not happen when you mix them.

PRIMARY AND SECONDARY COLOURS

Red, blue and yellow cannot be produced by mixing other colours, so they are called the primary colours. When mixed in pairs, these make the secondary colours: green

from blue and yellow; purple from blue and red; orange from red and yellow. But there is a slight complication here because the primary colours are not absolute – if you look at the starter palette below you will see that there are three different versions of each blue and yellow and two of red.

So before you begin to mix secondaries, you need to know which are the best primary colours to choose to mix the exact shade you want. All colours have different biases, or leanings towards other colours. Of the two reds in the starter palette, for example, one (cadmium red) is vivid and slightly yellow, while the other (alizarin crimson) leans towards blue. To mix bright secondaries you must choose the two primaries that are biased towards each other. Thus ultramarine (red biased) and alizarin crimson make a good purple, but ultramarine and cadmium red do not. For more muted secondaries, choose primaries which have an opposing bias.

Making bright mixtures
The mixtures shown here have all been made from two primary colours which have a bias towards each other. The resulting colours (secondaries) are all vivid, excepting the olive green.

Making subtle mixtures
Here primaries which have an opposite bias combine to make more muted mixtures.

Mixing browns and greys
Different permutations of the primary colours can produce a wide range of tertiary colours – browns, greys and muted greens. The proportion of each colour will depend on the mixture you are aiming at and on the strength of the individual colours – some pigments are stronger than others.

A STARTER PALETTE

The vast range of colours produced by paint manufacturers can be very bewildering for the beginner. How do you choose from this profusion, and how many colours do you need? In fact you don't need very many because you generally have to mix colours to produce equivalents to those you see in the real world. This suggested palette contains twelve colours, which may be over-generous – some of the great watercolourists of the past used no more than three or four.

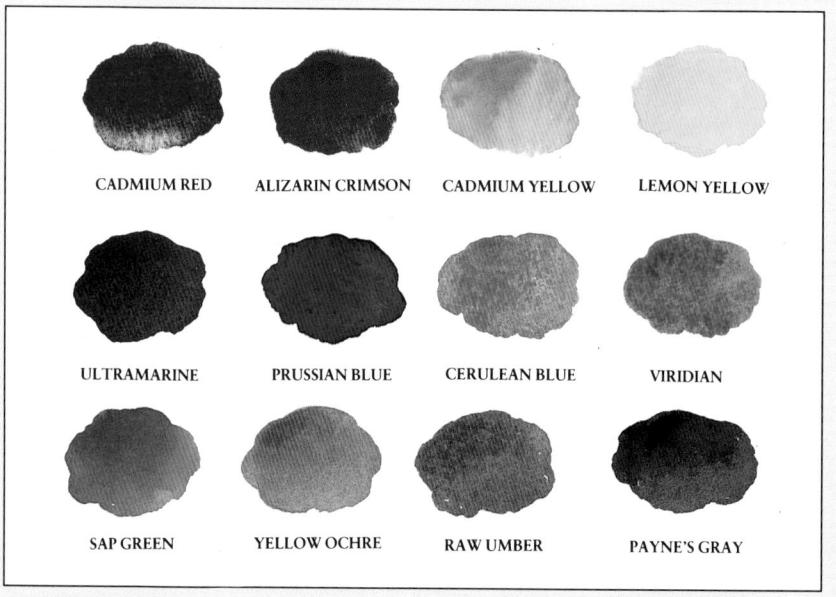

CADMIUM RED	ALIZARIN CRIMSON	CADMIUM YELLOW	LEMON YELLOW
ULTRAMARINE	PRUSSIAN BLUE	CERULEAN BLUE	VIRIDIAN
SAP GREEN	YELLOW OCHRE	RAW UMBER	PAYNE'S GRAY

CADMIUM RED   MIXTURE   CADMIUM YELLOW   ULTRAMARINE   MIXTURE   ALIZARIN CRIMSON   LEMON YELLOW   MIXTURE   PRUSSIAN BLUE

CADMIUM YELLOW   MIXTURE   ULTRAMARINE   CERULEAN BLUE   MIXTURE   LEMON YELLOW

LEMON YELLOW   MIXTURE   ALIZARIN CRIMSON   PRUSSIAN BLUE   MIXTURE   CADMIUM RED   LEMON YELLOW   MIXTURE   ULTRAMARINE

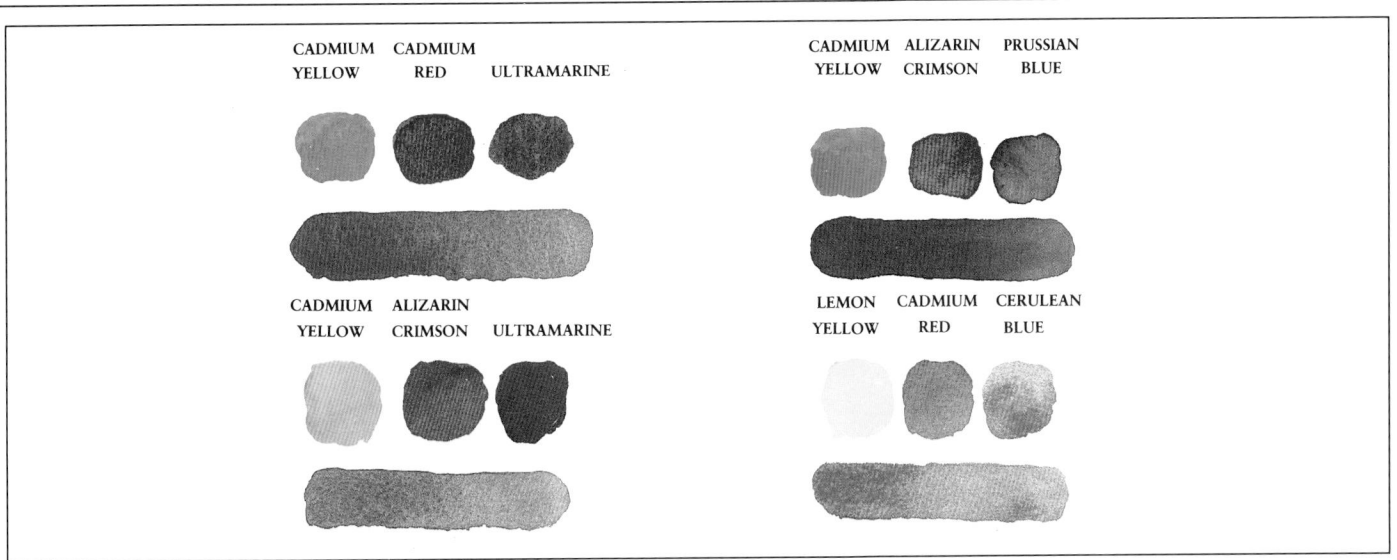

CADMIUM YELLOW   CADMIUM RED   ULTRAMARINE   CADMIUM YELLOW   ALIZARIN CRIMSON   PRUSSIAN BLUE

CADMIUM YELLOW   ALIZARIN CRIMSON   ULTRAMARINE   LEMON YELLOW   CADMIUM RED   CERULEAN BLUE

TERTIARY COLOURS

A secondary colour is a mixture of two other colours; when a third colour is added, the result is known as a tertiary colour. These are the so-called neutrals – the browns, beiges and "coloured greys" which play an important part in painting. There is no recipe for mixing these colours because there are so many possible ways of achieving them, but an interesting and varied range can be created simply by mixing three primary colours in different proportions.

WHY MIX?

You may wonder why it is necessary to mix secondary and tertiary colours at all when there are so many ready-made greens, purples and browns. But even if you were to buy a whole manufacturer's range you would seldom have exactly the right colour; furthermore, mixed colours are more subtle and more convincing than bought ones simply because you are making them up yourself, in direct response to a subject.

It is not always necessary to mix completely from scratch. The starter palette contains two secondary colours (the two greens) and two tertiary ones (raw umber and Payne's gray), all of which form good foundations for mixtures and can sometimes even be used as they are in certain areas of a picture. However, you would be well advised to practise colour mixing as much as possible, making charts like the ones shown here, as this will give you the hands-on experience for which there is no substitute.

A PAINTING IN SIX PRIMARIES

Making colour charts like those shown on the previous pages will help you to devise useful colour mixtures, giving you valuable experience in handling the medium; but the best way to learn to paint is to do it – that is, to paint an actual subject, choosing and mixing the colours accordingly. The idea behind this exercise is to discover whether you can make all the secondary and tertiary colours that you need for your work by using only the primary colours – two reds, three blues and three yellows.

You can choose any subject that appeals to you, but don't make it too complicated. You could set up a simple still life like the one shown here or, if you like to paint landscape, you could work from a photograph. Another alternative would be to copy a painting you like from a book of reproductions. There is nothing wrong with learning by copying. In this case, as you are only using six colours, your copy won't be exact; it will be what is known as a "transcription".

COLOURS USED *cadmium red, alizarin crimson, cadmium yellow, lemon yellow, ultramarine, Prussian blue*

1 *Having begun with a light brush drawing in yellow, the artist now paints in the shadow beneath the plate. This warm colour, mixed from cadmium red with small touches of ultramarine and lemon yellow, will later be modified by other colours laid on top.*

2 *The lemons present no problems, and the colours for these first washes do not require mixing. The lighter areas are pale lemon yellow, and the darker ones a stronger solution of cadmium yellow. Again, shadows will be added at a later stage.*

3 *Here the amount of water added to the colours is crucial. The paler pink at the top of the apple is well-watered alizarin crimson; beside this is a slightly stronger wash of the same colour, while for the body of the apple the crimson is more concentrated. Now a little blue is added to darken the red and tone it down slightly.*

4 The grey for the plate is mixed from ultramarine with small additions of lemon yellow and alizarin crimson, while the limes are mainly lemon yellow and Prussian blue, with light overlays of ultramarine for the shadows. These have been painted wet into wet so that they merge gently into the greens.

5 The same grey as that used for the plate is now washed over the original pinkish colour seen in Step 1. In watercolour work, colours are not only mixed in the paintbox or palette, they can also be modified and altered on the paper by laying one wash over another.

6 (Below) Final touches were added to darken the shadowed side of the lemon with a well-diluted mixture of ultramarine, lemon yellow and cadmium red, and to build up the forms of the other fruit with darker shadows. It is usually wise to avoid combining more than three colours, as this can make the mixture muddy; the majority of the mixtures here are of only two colours.

LAYING WASHES

Basically, watercolour painting is the process of building up a picture through a series of washes of paint diluted with water. A wash can cover the whole of the paper, half of it (perhaps for a sky) or just a small part; it can be roughly defined as colour that covers a wider area than an individual brushstroke could. In the later stages of a painting, definition may be added with small brushmarks or fine lines, but the washes come first and, because they are central to painting in watercolour, the first skill you must master is that of laying a completely even wash of colour.

MIXING COLOUR FOR A WASH

Washes must be laid quickly to prevent hard edges from forming. You cannot stop to make up more colour, so you must ensure that you have enough – washes use up a surprising amount of paint. The paint should be added to the water, not vice versa, but don't start with a large amount of water, or you could waste a good deal of paint achieving a strong enough mix. Instead, put a small amount of water into a saucer, palette or paintbox, pick up some colour with a moistened brush and stir it into the water. If it looks too light, add more paint, and if too dark add more water, repeating the process until you have the depth of colour you require. Stir the paint in well with the brush each time so that the particles of pigment are thoroughly dissolved and there are none left on the brush, otherwise you will have unsightly

DAVID CURTIS
SAILING BOATS
(Below) *The clear, pale sky behind the boats is achieved with a flat wash of watercolour.*

![Sailing boats watercolour painting by David Curtis]

Flat wash on dry paper

1 *The wash has been mixed in a jar rather than a paintbox because it is intended to cover a large area. Watercolour dries much lighter than it appears when wet, so the colour is tested on a spare piece of paper and allowed to dry before the wash is laid.*

2 *The board, on which the paper has been stretched with gumstrip, is propped at a slight angle, and the brush is taken smoothly from one side to the other.*

3 *Several successive bands of colour have now been laid. The angle of the board encourages the paint to flow downwards into each new band, so there are no perceptible boundaries.*

streaks of colour. Before laying the wash, check the colour by painting some on a spare piece of paper and letting it dry. Watercolour becomes much lighter as it dries, and the colour may not be what you originally expected.

LAYING THE WASH

The kind of brush you use is a matter of personal preference. Some artists like a large round brush, others prefer a flat one, and some eschew brushes altogether and lay washes with a sponge. Whichever "tool" you use the method is the same. Unless you are using very heavy paper it should first be stretched on a board and propped at a slight angle. The brush (or sponge) is then swept right across the paper from one side to the other; as soon as this first band of colour is in place, the brush is recharged and another band laid below, slightly overlapping the first. This process is repeated until the whole area is covered.

The tilt of the board encourages the paint to run down the paper so that each new "line" of colour mingles with the one above. Some artists like to dampen the paper with clean water before laying a wash, to encourage the colours to blend and to avoid any lines forming between bands. It is worth trying out both methods in order to discover which you prefer.

Flat wash on damp paper

1 *The paper is first dampened all over with a small natural sponge, which is a vital piece of equipment in watercolour work.*

2 *The way the paint runs down the damp paper can be alarming initially, but it will dry perfectly flat. This is a quick, effective method for covering large areas.*

Laying a flat wash with a sponge

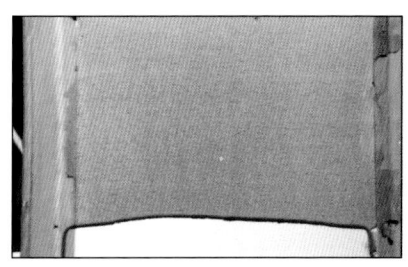

1 *Again working on damp paper, the sponge is taken from one side to the other. At this stage it is hard to believe that it will dry flat.*

2 *But it has. Because the paper was dampened, the darker areas of colour have flowed into the lighter ones, and the earlier irregularities have completely disappeared.*

Laying a gradated wash

1 *A band of full-strength colour is laid across the paper as usual; for each successive band the brush is dipped into the water and then into the paint mixture.*

2 *For artists who are interested in landscape painting this is the most useful type of wash, particularly for skies, which are usually lighter at the bottom.*

Laying a variegated wash

1 *Three colours are to be used and have been mixed up separately. The green touches the blue above so that the two colours blend together with no hard edges.*

2 *On this occasion the board is held flat and the paper is dry. The effect relies on the colours remaining distinct; on damp paper they would flow into one another and mix.*

GRADATED WASHES

Skies are darker at the top than the bottom and a colour wash should reflect this. Laying gradated washes, as they are called, is more difficult than laying flat ones; the need to make the colours progressively weaker or stronger can result in a stripy effect if you are not careful. You can work from light to dark, adding more paint for each band, but it is much easier to control the effect if you begin with the full-strength colour and add more water each time. If you want a wash which is darker at the bottom, simply turn the board upside down and work in the same way.

For each new band of colour, dip the brush into the water before dipping it into the paint in order to weaken the wash mixture by exactly the same amount each time. For a more obvious gradation, you can dip the brush twice into the water, or even use water alone for the second band, in which case the colour from the bottom of the first band will flow into the dampened area, thus creating a paler shadow of itself. Gradated washes must always be done on dry paper, otherwise the different strengths of colour will even out.

VARIEGATED WASHES

Washes frequently contain more than one colour. For instance, an area of grass in a landscape might vary from blue-green to yellow-green, or the sea could contain distinct colour fluctuations. In this case you need to mix in advance all the colours you require, washing your brush between each new colour to keep it pure.

Multi-coloured washes can be controlled quite precisely as long as you test all the colours on spare paper before you start. If you are aiming for a perfect blend of colours, with no obvious boundaries, it is best to work on dampened paper; a frequent feature of such washes, however, is that they are not regular and perfect – it all depends on what you want. You can also make exciting random effects by dropping new colours into a still-damp wash, a technique known as wet into wet, which is discussed later.

COMPLICATED EDGES

Laying a wash to cover a piece of paper entirely is easy enough once you have got the hang of it, but how do you lay a wash that starts and stops exactly where you want it to? You may, for example, want to lay a wash for a sky, below which is a complex skyline of buildings or trees which must stay clean, because it is to be painted in different colours.

In fact, this is much easier than it sounds, but it does rely on making a good drawing to establish exactly where to stop the wash. There are two ways of working and the one you choose depends on whether you like to lay washes on damp or dry paper. If you prefer the former, simply dampen the paper in the area of the wash only, taking a wet brush carefully around your drawn outlines. Lay the wash as usual and it will stop obediently at the dry paper. If you want to lighten the colour slightly and ensure a smooth and even texture, then dab it with blotting paper which will absorb some of the excess paint.

The other method is to work upside down, taking the colour around the edges first. If you want a wash which is darker at the top, leave the board to dry upside down and at an angle; the colour will flow down – that is, up in terms of your picture.

Tricky edges: method 1

1 *The wash is to be laid on the sky but not the hills, so the paper has been dampened in the sky area only. The paint stops flowing as soon as it reaches the edge of the dry paper.*

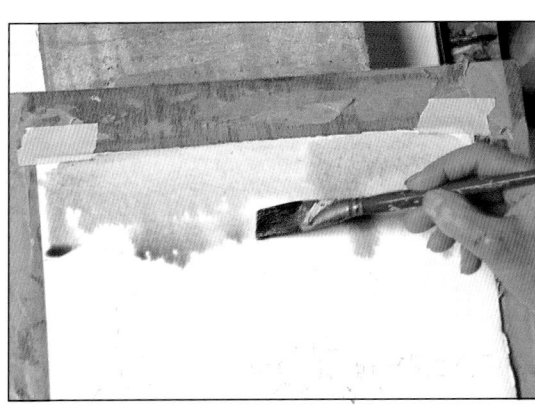

2 *Notice that the sky wash has dried completely flat. The paper is now dampened again, this time between the sky and the buildings, and a loose multi-coloured wash is laid.*

Tricky edges: method 2

1 *The board is turned upside down and a deep blue wash laid around the line of the roofs. A round brush with a good point is best for this method.*

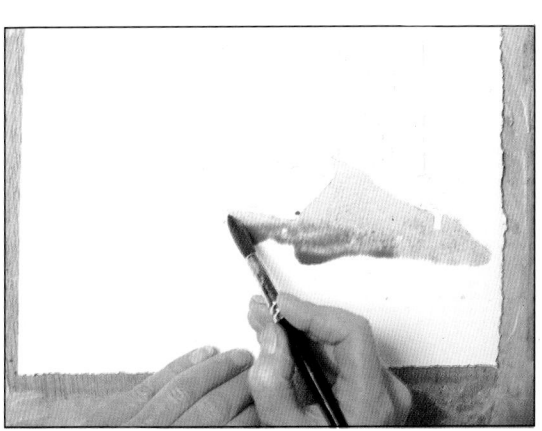

2 *The board has been tilted so that the paint flows downwards, that is, to the top of the sky area. It is left to dry in this position.*

MAKING AN UNDERDRAWING

Unless you are just making quick sketches or coloured "doodles" to try out techniques and colour effects, it is important to start your work with a plan of campaign, which means a drawing. This establishes where to place the first washes and which areas to reserve for highlights. Bear in mind too that it is not easy to make major corrections to watercolours, so an initial drawing will save frustration later on.

You may groan at the idea, because it prevents you from getting down to what most people regard as the fun part of the exercise, which is putting on the colour. Also, of course, it seems a waste of valuable painting time – if you are working out of doors, every second counts. You may find in such cases that it is better to make the drawing on one day and paint on the next. Changing light is less important when you are drawing than when you are painting.

Too elaborate a drawing is unnecessary and you should keep it faint, otherwise the pencil marks may show through the lighter areas of colour. Avoid shading and try to restrict yourself to outlines, while making sure that you know what the outlines mean. If you have to amend the drawing, erase the wrong lines as soon as you are confident that the drawing is correct. Take care over erasing as the surfaces of some papers become scuffed rather easily, causing unpleasant blotches when the paint is applied. Use a soft plastic eraser or a kneaded putty one, keeping the pressure light to avoid spoiling the paper surface.

Making a pencil drawing

1 *The artist is using a fairly soft pencil (4B). Anything harder than a 2B could indent the surface of the paper, and is less easy to erase if you make a mistake.*

2 (Right) *The drawing has been kept to outlines only, but the lines are strong enough to provide a guide for the applications of paint. If the drawing is too pale it will quickly become obscured by the first washes.*

Squaring up

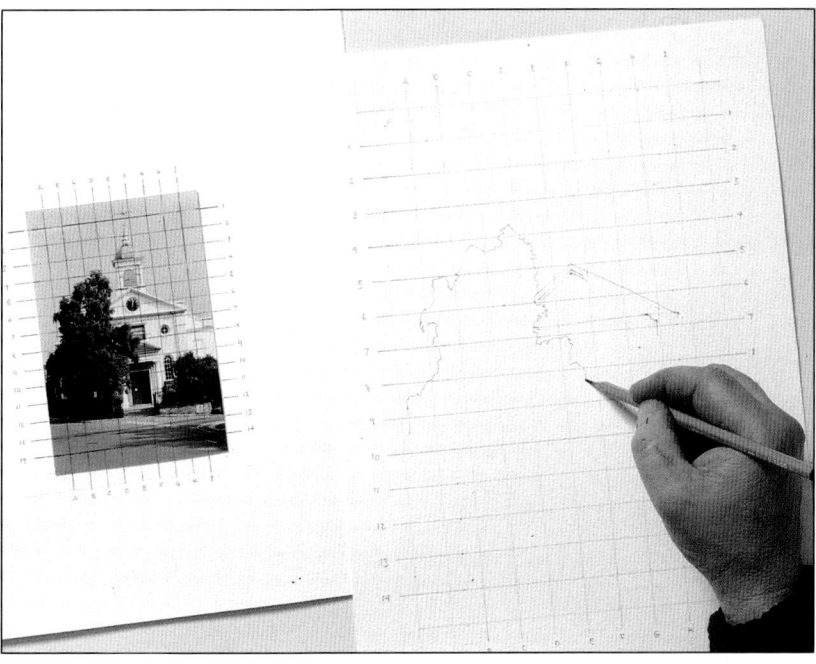

1 *A grid of squares has been drawn over the photograph, and a larger grid is now marked out on the paper. Numbering the squares is important, as it is easy to make mistakes when transferring the visual information.*

2 (Right) *Referring to the numbers and letters, the artist redraws the image, taking care to assess where each line intersects with a line on the grid.*

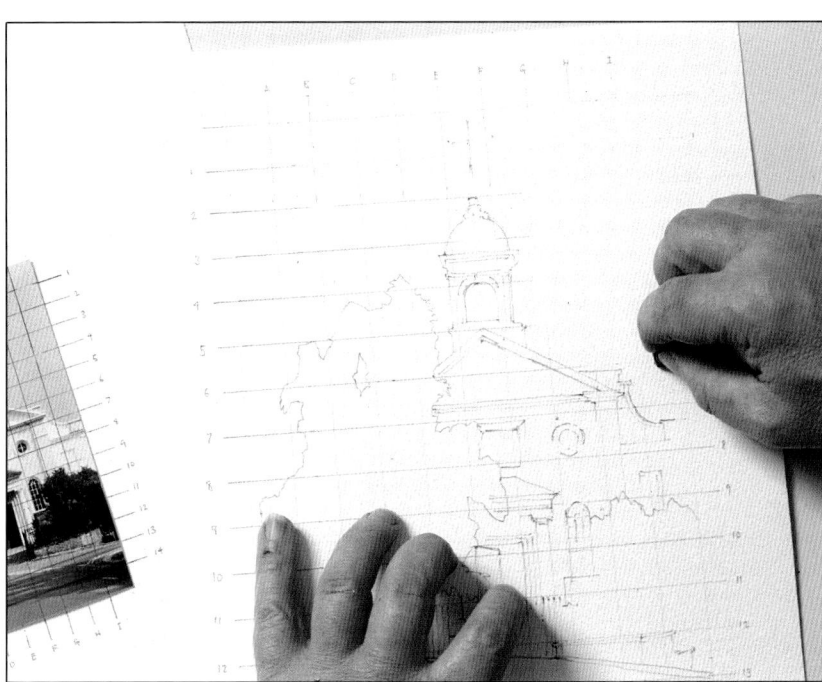

3 *The grid lines are erased in the areas which are to be light in the painting because they would show through pale washes. A putty eraser is used to avoid any risk of scuffing the paper.*

If you are working from a photograph (and don't be ashamed, because many artists do), you can enlarge the image and transfer it to the painting surface by a tried-and-tested method called squaring up. Using a ruler, draw a measured grid over the photograph and then another one, with larger squares, on the paper. You will have to work out the sizes of the squares mathematically according to the size you want your picture to be. For example, if those on the photograph are 1.3 cm (½ in) and those on the paper are 2.5 cm (1 in), the painting will be twice the size of the photograph. Once you have drawn the grids, simply transfer the information from one to the other, checking carefully to see where each line intersects a grid line. This is well worth the effort for any complicated subject, such as architecture, where one wrong angle can throw everything out. It is actually much easier for the eye to judge the exact angles of a subject by comparison with the straight right-angles of a grid.

WORKING WET ON DRY

Watercolour paints are transparent, and consequently paintings are built up in layers, working from light to dark. It is seldom possible to achieve a really dark colour with just one wash, because the paint must be diluted with water in order to spread, and the white of the paper will always show through to some extent. Thus the darkest colours are achieved by laying one wash over another until the required depth is achieved. This layering method, known as wet on dry because each wash must be fully dry before the next is added, is the "classic" watercolour technique. When each wash dries, it forms hard edges at the boundaries; these edges are a positive feature of wet-on-dry painting, adding crisp energy to the image.

The method relies for its success on careful planning. It is not wise to pile on too much colour; as a general rule you should limit yourself to not more than three overlaid washes, as otherwise the colours will begin to lose their clarity, becoming stirred up and muddy. Thus when you begin a painting you need to have a clear idea of what the finished work is to look like, as only in this way can you estimate the depth of colour you need for the first washes. Overlaid washes should always be restricted to relatively small areas of the picture.

You also need to plan the highlights. As you already know, the white in watercolour comes from the paper. White highlights are achieved by "reserving", which means leaving the shape as white paper and painting around it. Highlights are not always white, but areas of a light-coloured wash can be reserved in the same way, by leaving parts showing through overlaid washes. White highlights can be added in opaque paint, but for purity and sparkle you can't beat unblemished white paper.

Overlaid washes

1 *The reflective surface produces blues and whites among the browns, so the artist has begun with a grey-blue wash, slightly darker in the shadow areas, reserving the areas of pure white highlight by painting around them.*

2 *Each wash must be completely dry before the next one is painted on top, so a hairdryer is used to speed up the process. This is a very useful piece of equipment when working indoors.*

3 *The same light brown used for the top of the teapot is now introduced at the bottom. It is best to work from top to bottom whenever possible, to avoid smudging wet paint.*

6 (Above) *Shiny surfaces reflect light and shadow from their surroundings, creating very sharp and distinctly shaped areas of light and dark. The crispness produced by using the wet-on-dry technique is ideal for conveying these qualities in a painting.*

4 *A darker mixture of the same brown is used for the shadowed areas. Notice that, on the lid of the pot, an area of blue-grey formed by the brown painted over the blue in Step 3 has been carefully reserved as a highlight.*

5 *The darkest colours are left until the final stages and placed very carefully. These shadows, like the highlights, define the form of the object.*

WORKING WET INTO WET

This method, which involves applying new colours before the first ones have been allowed to dry, is often regarded as a "special" method, quite separate from the classic wet-on-dry technique. In fact, although some artists do paint whole pictures wet into wet, it is perhaps more usual to see the two methods used in conjunction with one another.

Painting wet into wet is enormously enjoyable. One of the delights of water-colour is its unpredictability, and here the medium is at its tantalizing best – you never know exactly what will happen. Surprisingly, when you drop one wet colour into another, they do not mix completely. The weight of water in the new brushstroke pushes the first layers of paint away slightly, so that the colours mingle and "bleed" into one another, while still remaining separate to an extent. This can create very exciting effects, which vary according to how wet the paint is, the kind of paper you use and

Working on dry paper

1 *Whether you work on pre-dampened or dry paper depends on how thorough you want the wet-into-wet effect to be. Here the artist needs a crisp edge at the top of the hills, and therefore uses dry paper.*

2 *Several applications of paint have by now made the paper thoroughly damp, and the green applied in the foreground spreads out and diffuses. To control the spread of colour, the artist applies the paint lightly, with the tip of the brush.*

Controlling the flow

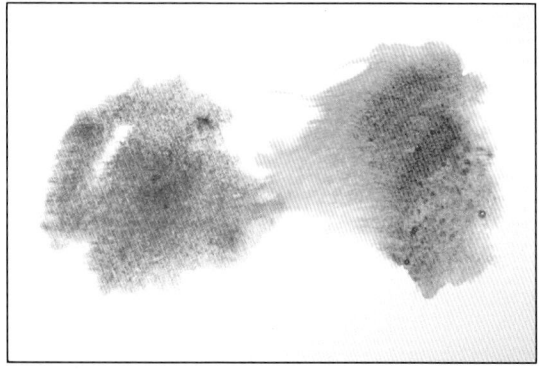

1 *The paper has been dampened, two colours laid side by side, and the paper lifted and tilted to the left so that the red runs into the blue.*

2 *(Right) A stronger blue has been dropped in at the top and the paper is now tilted so that the colours run down. The paper should normally be stretched for wet-into-wet work, but this is very heavy paper which does not buckle.*

3 *The paper has now been damped only in one area so that the blue paint does not spread below the boundary of the cloud. The tip of the brush is used to create a slightly streaky patch of sky.*

4 *(Above) The same method is used for the large cloud, with dark mauve-greys introduced into a lighter wet wash. Smaller, paler clouds are now touched in above the horizon, again with the tip of the brush.*

5 *(Left) The soft effect of the wet-into-wet painting is enhanced by the occasional crisp edges. Parts of the wall and the small tree have been painted wet on dry, while the cloud has formed a jagged edge where the wet paint met dry paper.*

the colours themselves (different pigments have different "behaviour patterns"). The main problem with the method is that you can't control it very precisely – the paint continues moving until it has dried, and you often find that you cannot preserve a particular effect. You can exert some control, however, by tilting the board so that the paint runs in a certain direction. Artists who paint extensively wet into wet will sometimes move the board around until they have achieved the flow of colours they want; they then use a hairdryer to hasten

the drying process and thus "freeze" the picture at a specific moment.

Wet into wet can create a lovely soft atmosphere and, for this reason, is often used for landscapes and weather effects. It can, however, look *too* soft, giving the painting a distinctly woolly and nebulous appearance, so sharper details are usually painted wet on dry as a final stage. You can also add an extra dimension to any subject by working wet into wet in small areas only, thus contrasting soft, blurred edges with the crisper ones made by wet-on-dry washes.

BRUSHWORK

People do not always think of brushwork in connection with watercolour. So much emphasis is placed on the importance of laying flat washes that this aspect of painting tends to be overlooked, but, although brushwork in general is less obvious in watercolour than in a thick, buttery medium like oil, it still has a place. Sometimes it is restricted to the final defining details in a painting. In a mainly wet-into-wet landscape, for example, some light flicks of the brush can suggest foreground grass or the branches of trees, in contrast to softer blends of colour elsewhere in the picture.

Brushwork is more important in the classic wet-on-dry method because of the possibilities presented by the hard edges formed by overlaid washes. These "washes" can take the form of individual brushmarks: perhaps small dabs to suggest the foliage of a tree; calligraphic squiggles to describe reflections in water, or sweeps with a broad brush to follow the direction of clouds in a

windswept sky. Some artists lay almost no conventional flat washes, constructing whole paintings by means of a network of interconnected brushmarks.

Obviously different brushes make different marks, so try to discover their capabilities by practising "drawing" with a brush. You can make a wide range of marks with just one brush if you vary the way you hold it and the amount of pressure you apply. Most people tend to hold a brush as though they were writing, gripping it firmly near the ferrule, but, although this gives maximum control, it can limit the artist's expressive style. Try holding it nearer the top and varying the pressure from heavy to light, flicking it at the end of a stroke. See what happens if you use a flat brush and twist it in mid-stroke, or draw out a brushstroke as far as you can so that the brush is progressively starved of paint. This kind of doodling is never a waste of time, as you will be training your hand, albeit unconsciously.

Drawing with paint

1 *The artist has chosen to work on a smooth-surfaced watercolour paper, which enables her to combine strong brushmarks with softer wet-into-wet painting. She begins with broad strokes, letting the colours run together slightly.*

2 *The first applications of paint have now begun to dry, but are still damp enough for the next brushstrokes to spread slightly and soften.*

3 *Crisp strokes of almost undiluted colour are now worked wet on dry over the softer brushmarks. Notice the position of the brush; instead of pulling it downwards in the usual way, the artist uses an upward flick.*

5 *A broader effect suggesting the dark green foliage is produced by flooding dark green paint into lighter green, in a modified wet-into-wet technique.*

4 (Above) *At the top of the picture, the succession of criss-crossing brushmarks, where the first colours show through the later ones, creates a lively impression of light and movement.*

6 (Below) *The small backrun at the top of the tree and the jagged edges on the tree trunk and foliage formed as the washes dried out; these are typical semi-accidents which occur during watercolour work. Experienced painters exploit such effects rather than trying to correct them, and here they enhance the lively, edgy quality of the picture.*

LIFTING OUT

As we have seen earlier, highlights in watercolour are normally created by painting around them. There is, however, another method, which involves putting on paint and then removing it. Highlights made by the classic reserving method have crisp, clear edges, but often a softer, more diffuse effect is required. For example, clouds or matt-surfaced objects do not have sharp highlights and would look unrealistic if painted in this way. In such cases, lifting out is the method you need.

It is beautifully easy; all you do is lay down the paint and, before it has dried, dab into it or wipe it with a very slightly damp sponge, a rag, a piece of kitchen paper or blotting paper – anything absorbent in fact. If you have ever worried about how to create the effect of white clouds in a blue sky without laboriously painting around the shapes (which looks unnatural anyway), your problems are solved. Simply lay a gradated wash and then dab into it or, for windclouds, sweep across the paper with your chosen implement. More complex colour effects can be created by lifting out one colour to reveal another. For the soft dappling of foliage, for example, you could lay a dark green wash over a lighter one which has been allowed to dry, then lift out some of the darker colour.

Small, soft highlights, such as those on matt-surfaced objects or on distant water in a landscape, can be made by allowing a cotton bud (swab) or virtually dry paint-brush to suck up some of the colour where you want the highlight to be. You can even lift out dry paint in small areas, using a firmer pressure and slightly more water. Alternatively, you can scrape into the paint with a blade. This scratching technique is commonly used for tiny, fine lines, such as those created by light on blades of grass.

Lifting out clouds

1 *Having laid a pale blue wash, allowed it to dry and then painted a multi-coloured wash on top, the artist uses a crumpled piece of kitchen paper to dab into wet paint.*

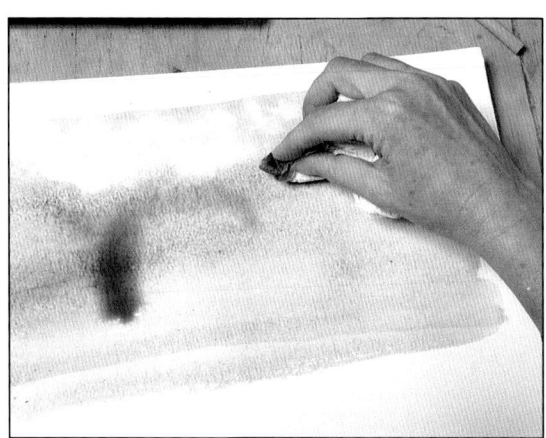

2 *To darken the undersides of the clouds, more colour has been laid on, wet into wet, and is partially removed again with kitchen paper.*

3 *The effect is very realistic and has been achieved with the minimum of time and effort. The soft clouds at the top contrast with the irregular edges formed when the darker washes dried out.*

Lifting out dry paint

1 *A series of green washes has been painted over a dry yellow one, with small areas of the yellow reserved for the sharper highlights.*

2 (Right) *A cotton bud (swab) dipped into water is now used to work into the green paint, creating much softer highlights than can be achieved by reserving.*

3 *Finally, tiny highlights are made by scratching into the dry paint with a scalpel blade. This must always be done at a final stage in the painting because it breaks up the paper surface, making it impossible to lay colour on top.*

4 (Right) *The lifting-out method is ideal for the soft, diffused highlights seen on foliage or matt-surfaced objects, but is most effective when contrasted with the crisper edges achieved by reserving areas of the painting.*

MASKING

Reserving highlights by painting around them is ideal if the required shape is reasonably large and clearly defined, but often the highlights may be small and intricate, in which case it is helpful to use masking fluid. Some watercolourists disdain the use of such methods, regarding them as "mechanical" or "tricksy", but others find them indispensable.

The great advantage of masking is that it removes the worry and allows you to paint more freely. If you have to think constantly about not taking the paint over little shapes which you want to reserve, there is a danger that your work may become tight and fussy; masking fluid allows you to work as broadly and splashily as you like, knowing that those areas are protected.

Masking fluid is a viscous solution sold in small bottles. It is either white or yellow, the latter being the best choice because you can see where you are putting it on. It is applied with a brush and, when dry, washes are laid on top. When these too are dry, the fluid is removed by rubbing with a finger or a plastic eraser. Wash the brush immediately because, once dry, the fluid is very difficult to remove from the hairs – and don't use your most expensive brush.

Highlights with masking fluid

1 *Here the artist is using masking fluid to reserve small areas suggesting dappled light. She starts with a pencil drawing and then paints on the masking fluid with a small brush.*

Painting white shapes

Masking fluid not only provides a convenient means of reserving white paper for highlights, but can also be used in a more positive way to make distinctive brushmarks of white. Being thick, it holds the marks of the brush very effectively, as you can see from these examples, where the fluid was removed after the paint had dried. You are thus virtually painting with white, in a way that is otherwise impossible with watercolour alone.

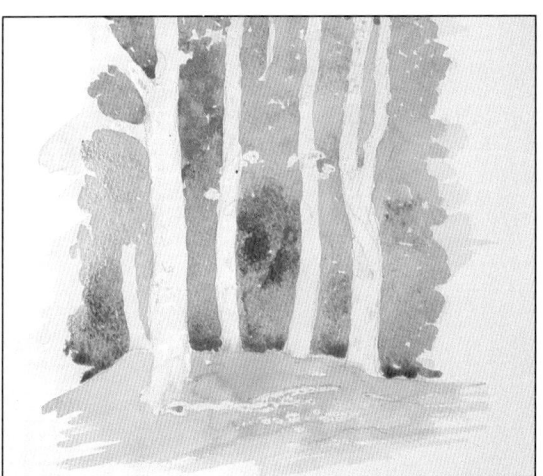

2 *A light blue-grey wash is taken over the whole area of tree trunks and foliage and allowed to dry before further greens and yellows are painted, largely wet into wet.*

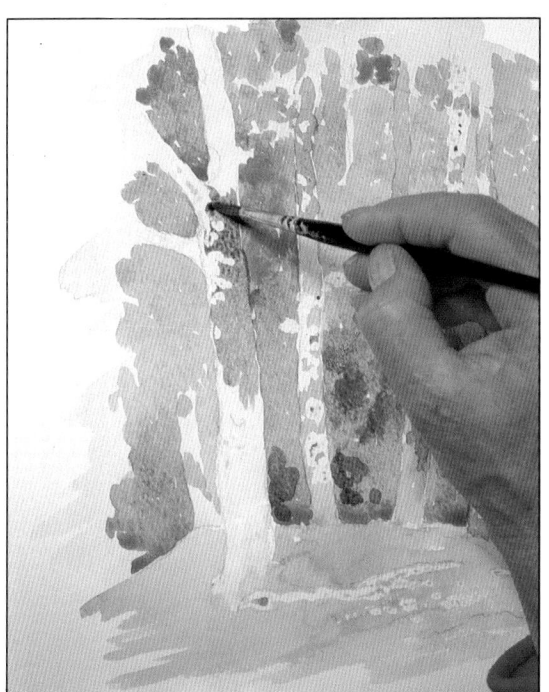

3 *The colours of the foliage must be kept separate from those of the tree trunks, so the first colours were dried with a hairdryer. Browns are now painted over the masking fluid.*

4 (Right) *The fluid is removed by rubbing with a finger. The paint must be perfectly dry before this is done, so again a hairdryer was used.*

5 (Above) *When the masking fluid is taken off, you often find that some of the white highlights are too stark. In this case they have been left as white on the two left-hand tree trunks, but slightly darkened elsewhere; light yellow washes were laid over the leaves in the centre and on the lighter patch of foreground.*

USING OPAQUE PAINT

Watercolour has not always been used as a transparent medium in the past, nor is it always used as one today. Artists such as Albrecht Dürer in the Renaissance period and J.M.W. Turner in the 19th century used watercolour which was similar to today's gouache paints. Many of today's artists use gouache and watercolour together, or mix their colours with a little opaque white, which gives them body while still preserving much of their translucent quality (opaque watercolour is sometimes referred to as "body colour").

Opaque paint, like masking fluid, is frowned upon by some purists, who regard it as cheating, but this is nonsense. The point of painting is to exploit your medium to the full, to gain the effects you want; if you can do this by adding opaque white, then go ahead and do it. It is the perfect method for atmospheric weather effects, for example, such as cloud-shrouded hills or the soft lights on water.

You can add an extra dimension to your work by using coloured paper, whether or not you are adding white to the paint. Working over a base colour gives you a start in the process of building up the colours; it is particularly well suited to any paintings which are to be relatively dark overall, without bright highlights. It is now possible to buy coloured watercolour papers, but they are not easily available, so you might consider trying some of the papers made for pastel work, which come in an extensive colour range. Stretch them first, however, as they are thinner than most watercolour papers.

Working on tinted paper

1 *The artist is using a paper whose surface is rather similar to the Ingres paper used for pastel work, but it is thicker and does not buckle when wet. He makes a careful drawing of the buildings within the landscape before putting on any colour.*

2 *The secret behind an effective opaque-watercolour technique is to add white to the paint only where necessary, and to use it sparingly. Here white has been used for the sky, but the darker paint now being applied is pure watercolour.*

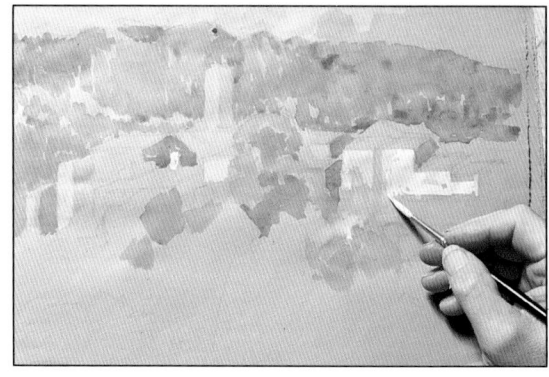

3 *For the houses, white with a small addition of crimson is painted into pure white, wet into wet, to create a slight blending of colours. Wet-into-wet effects are less dramatic and unpredictable with opaque paint, because it runs less freely.*

4 *Again opaque white is mixed with watercolour, as it was for the roofs of the houses. The white used is gouache paint, which the artist finds more satisfactory than the Chinese white sold for watercolour work.*

5 *In the final stages, a small brush was used to outline the roofs and paint in details of windows; now the foreground foliage is built up with small washes and overlaid brushstrokes of pure watercolour. The darker colours have been kept transparent throughout.*

6 (Above) *The finished picture is delightfully delicate and fresh, retaining the translucent qualities associated with watercolour. The colour of the paper, deliberately left to show between brushstrokes in the background and foreground, plays an important part in the overall colour scheme.*

TEXTURING METHODS

It can be hard to know where to start when describing texture in a fluid medium like watercolour. How, for instance, do you give the impression of a shingle beach or a cornfield without painting every pebble or cornhead? In fact there are a good many special techniques to hand. One is dry brush which, as its name implies, means working with the minimum of paint on the brush so that it only partially covers the paper. This method is often used for grass, the hazy effect of distant trees or the fur of animals. The best brush to use is a flat one, with the hairs slightly splayed out between thumb and forefinger and then dabbed onto blotting paper or absorbent kitchen paper to remove the excess paint.

Another popular method is spattering or flicking paint onto the paper with an old toothbrush. The toothbrush is loaded with colour and held above the work; the handle

Dry-brushed grasses

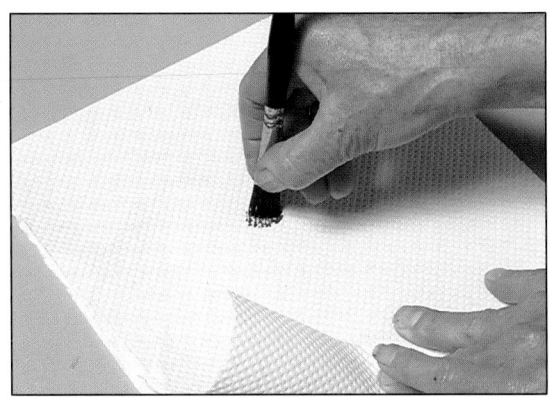

1 *As the name of the method implies, the brush must be fairly dry so, after dipping it into the paint, the artist dabs it onto a piece of kitchen paper to remove the surplus paint.*

2 *Using a square-ended brush, she splays the hairs out slightly and then gently drags the brush over the paper, creating a series of fine lines.*

3 *(Left) One layer of dry brushing has been laid over another to suggest the different directions in which the marsh grasses lean.*

Toothbrush spatter

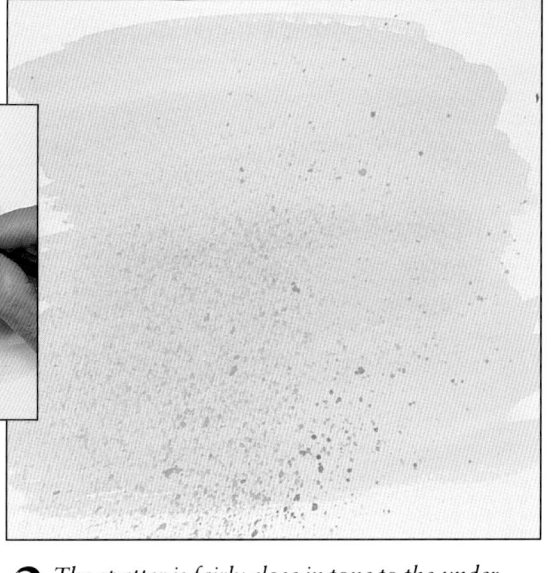

1 *A toothbrush is loaded with paint, and a pencil is pulled across the bristles to release a fine spray.*

2 *The spatter is fairly close in tone to the underlying wash and avoids being too obtrusive – it is easy to overdo this method.*

Paintbrush spatter

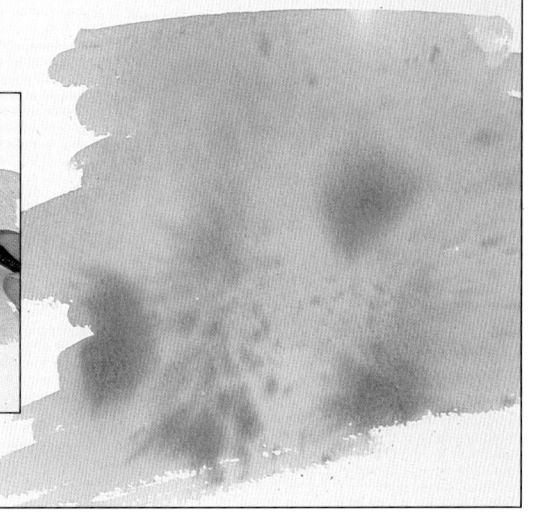

1 *This time dark paint is spattered into a light green wash using a bristle brush tapped against a pencil, producing larger droplets.*

2 *As the spattering was done wet into wet, the darker colour has spread out and blended to some extent with the lighter one.*

Salt spatter

1 *This technique works best on a non-absorbent paper, and here smooth (hot-pressed) watercolour paper is used. The salt is dropped into a wash and begins to absorb the water immediately.*

2 *(Right) These examples show some of the different effects which can be achieved; they vary according to the colour used, the wetness of the wash and the closeness of the crystals.*

of a brush, a knife or your thumbnail is drawn quickly across it to release a spray of droplets. This technique is very effective for suggesting texture without describing it too literally, but it should not be overdone, nor should it look too obtrusive. If you are spattering over a pale wash, perhaps for a sandy beach, don't make the spattered colour too dark or it will look artificial. Spattering can also be used in a purely decorative way, to create an area of colour with a stippled appearance.

A particularly exciting method, ideal for the texture of old pitted rocks or crumbling walls, is salt spatter, which involves dropping crystals of coarse sea salt into wet paint. The salt granules absorb the water while "pushing away" the pigment, leaving a pattern of pale, crystalline shapes when they are removed. The effects vary according to how wet the paint is and which colours you use – some pigments are "heavier" than others and do not move so readily. For the best results, apply the salt just after the wash has lost its sheen, which indicates that it is beginning to dry. The salt itself takes a long time to dry, but it is worth persevering with the technique.

WAX RESIST

In one way this technique is similar to that of using masking fluid. Both involve creating a block which prevents the paint from reaching the paper, but wax resist gives a very different effect. It is based on the mutual antipathy of oil (the wax) and water (the paint). If you scribble over paper with a household candle or wax crayon and then apply washes, the paint will slide off the wax. Unlike masking fluid, however, which leaves perfect shapes when removed, the wax creates a subtler, lightly speckled effect. This is because watercolour paper is textured, so the wax adheres only to the top of the grain, unless you draw very heavily indeed with the candle or crayon.

Wax resist is a simple technique which can yield quite beautiful results. It is often used in landscape, for skies lightly broken by clouds or the gentle gleam of water on lakes, rivers and seas. It also provides yet another way of describing texture. The roughened surface of an old building, a crumbling cliff or an ancient gnarled tree, for example, can be quickly and easily suggested with a light application of wax under loose wet-into-wet washes.

If you want a coloured resist, you can use wax-oil crayons or the new oil bars, which serve the purpose very well. You can make the wax underdrawing as simple or as complex as you like. Some artists build up paintings in layers, applying crayon, then paint and then more crayon, sometimes even scratching into the wax before putting on more paint. It is an exciting method to try as it contains an element of surprise – you never quite know what will happen.

Watercolour and oil bar

1 *This artist uses wax resist a good deal in her work, building up effects by means of a layering technique. She has begun with loose watercolour washes and now scribbles over the dry paint with a transparent oil bar.*

Types of wax

The final results depend on the texture of the paper, the pressure applied and the kind of wax used. A household candle was used for the first example and an oil bar for the other two. More delicate lines can be made with a wax-oil crayon.

2 *As the watercolour is applied on top, it slides off the wax, leaving small blobs and speckles. This method is often used to suggest texture.*

3 *A further application of oil bar has been followed by another watercolour wash, which is smeared down the paper to create an effect of brushstrokes.*

4 *While the paint in the foreground is still wet, a craft knife is used to scratch into both wax and paint. Dark lines are created where the wax is removed, as the paint seeps into the slightly scuffed paper surface.*

5 *A lighter scratching method is used for the sky, but in this case the effect is different because the knife removes the layer of watercolour on top of the wax, leaving white marks.*

6 *(Right) The artist has not attempted a precise representation of the landscape features; the wax resist in the foreground suggests water without describing it literally. Her approach is impressionistic and, to a large extent, she allows the painting itself to dictate her procedure.*

LINE & WASH

This technique, which combines drawing and painting, has been in use for a long time, but has lost none of its appeal. Traditionally it was employed by illustrators – as it still is today – as a means of introducing colour into what were basically drawings, usually in pen and ink. Nowadays artists exploit the technique of line and wash in more personal and often highly inventive ways.

Line and wash is essentially a mixed-media technique and, as in all such work, it is important to try to integrate the two media to create a unified image. Thus it is not always wise to begin with the drawing, or at any rate to take the drawing to a finished stage, before putting on colour. Generally the best and most "painterly" effects are created by developing the two side by side, adding more colour and more line as the picture demands.

You don't have to use pen for line and wash – watercolour is often combined with pencil drawing, the pencil lines providing detail and touches of definition. Pencil and watercolour marry very well together, as pencil gives a gentler and less assertive line than pen.

However, on the whole, pen is the implement most often used, so if you want to try this technique you will need to experiment with different pens, of which there is a bewilderingly large range on the market. You can use fine fibre-tipped and felt-tipped pens (but make sure they are non-fading), fountain pens or dip pens. For the beginner, the latter are probably the best, as a holder with interchangeable nibs is relatively inexpensive. Waterproof ink is normally used, but it is worth trying water-soluble ink too. This runs slightly when the watercolour washes are laid on top, which can be an effective way of softening the line.

Pen and watercolour

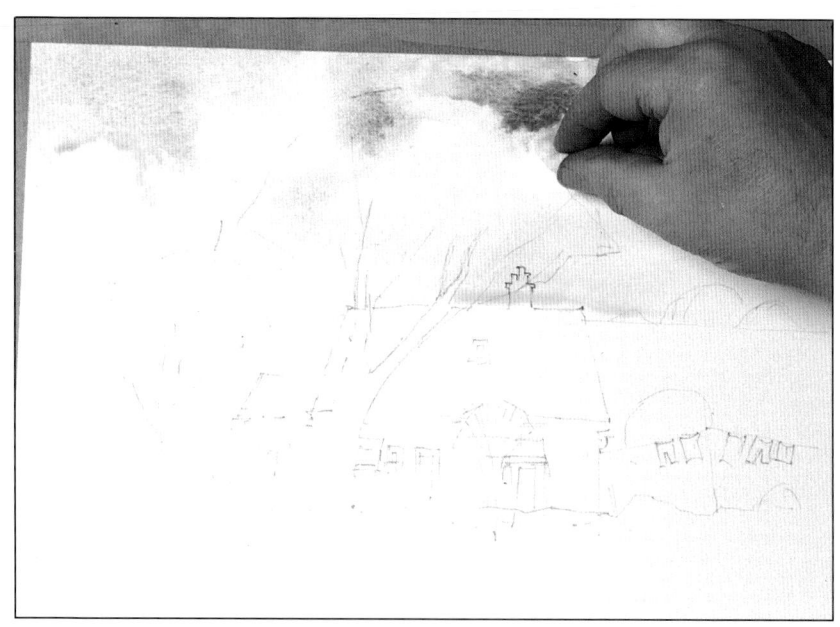

1 *The artist likes to develop line and colour together, so he has begun by making a pencil drawing to provide some guidelines for the first washes, which he applies loosely, wet into wet.*

2 *With the washes now dry, he draws with a pen, using waterproof ink. He keeps the line drawing to a minimum at this stage of the work.*

3 *The drawing has been considerably strengthened with bold lines and areas of hatching and cross-hatching. To avoid giving too much prominence to the linear element, the artist now applies darker colour.*

4 The area in front of the house is defined with further pen work. Notice how the wet-into-wet washes in the foreground have dried with hard, irregular edges, complementing the pen lines.

5 A succession of washes has been laid over the large tree, again with the paint used loosely and freely; final touches are added with a finer nib than that used previously.

6 (Above) When the entire drawing is done at the beginning, pen-and-wash work can become rather tight and fussy, giving the effect of a "filled-in drawing". The artist has avoided this pitfall and integrated the drawing and painting media, while still providing a good contrast between linearity and boldly applied colour.

BACKRUNS

If you have ever tried to work into a wash before it is dry, you may have come across the phenomenon of the backrun. The new paint seeps into the old, creating an odd blotch with hard, jagged edges – some people call it a cauliflower for obvious reasons. Normally backruns cause alarm and despondency because you may have to abandon a whole piece of paper, or at least wash the area down with a sponge and begin again.

However, a very important part of watercolour work is learning how to exploit accidental effects of this nature – watercolours are never totally predictable. Some artists induce backruns deliberately, or simply allow them to happen and then leave them alone because they improve the painting. The effects they create are quite different from those made by more conventional means, and the strange shapes are often highly suggestive. For example, a backrun in a sky can often look like a cloud, possibly suggesting a different treatment

from the one you originally had in mind, while one in the foreground might provide the perfect touch of additional interest. In flower painting, backruns are particularly useful, often resembling the shapes of petals and flowers.

WATERCOLOUR PALETTE

WATERCOLOUR PANS

Backruns cannot be controlled with much precision, but you are not altogether at the mercy of events. You can make them happen at will if you always use paint which has a higher water content than the original colour (thick paint on thin will not work). You can tilt the board, as in any wet-into-wet work, and then use a hairdryer to "stop" the run when you are satisfied with the effect, but remember that wet-into-wet paint goes on moving until it dries.

Accidental backruns

These examples show what can happen when you panic and try to work back into a wash. In the first, the wash was very wet; in the second, it appeared dry but was not.

Deliberate backruns

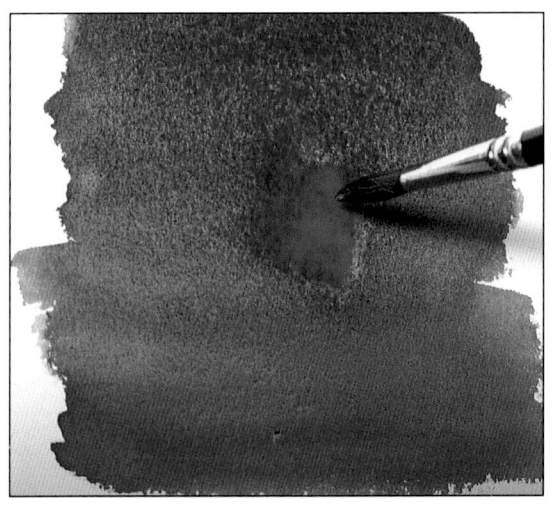

1 *A dark indigo wash is laid first, and a slightly more watery solution of alizarin crimson is then dropped into the wet paint. It begins to spread immediately.*

2 *The paint will continue to move until it is fully dry. At this stage the first wash has begun to dry at the edges, but the central area is still wet, and the crimson continues to bleed into the darker colour.*

3 *Yellow is now dropped into the centre; this in turn pushes the crimson away to create a pale area within the darker colours.*

4 *(Right) Finally the paper is allowed to dry out and a light crimson applied wet on dry, followed by a darker crimson worked wet into wet. A variety of flower-like effects can be produced in this way.*

PAINT ADDITIVES

The pigment used to make watercolours is bound with a gum called gum arabic, which can also be used as a painting medium; it is sold in most good art shops. A little gum mixed with water (known as gum water) makes the paint more lustrous and less runny, giving it extra body. This allows you to build up an area of the picture in small separate brushstrokes which do not merge together. It is thus useful for any area of a picture where you want a lot of precise detail, particularly if you intend to use dark colours, which can otherwise become muddy and dull. It is also useful for lifting out dry paint. If you lay a colour mixed with gum water over another paler wash and let it dry before working into areas with a wet brush, the top layer of paint will come away very easily because the water dissolves the gum, revealing the paint beneath.

Using gum water

1 *The artist began with conventional water and paint washes, and has painted the trees with dark green paint mixed with gum water (about two parts of water to one of gum). Notice the richness of the colours and how each brushstroke remains separate.*

2 *Gum arabic also facilitates the lifting-out technique. The gum is water-soluble, so a wet brush dabbed into the paint removes the top layer.*

3 *A damp rag is dabbed lightly into the paint to create softer, more diffuse highlights. Note how the original yellow wash remains intact; this is because gum water was not used for the first colours.*

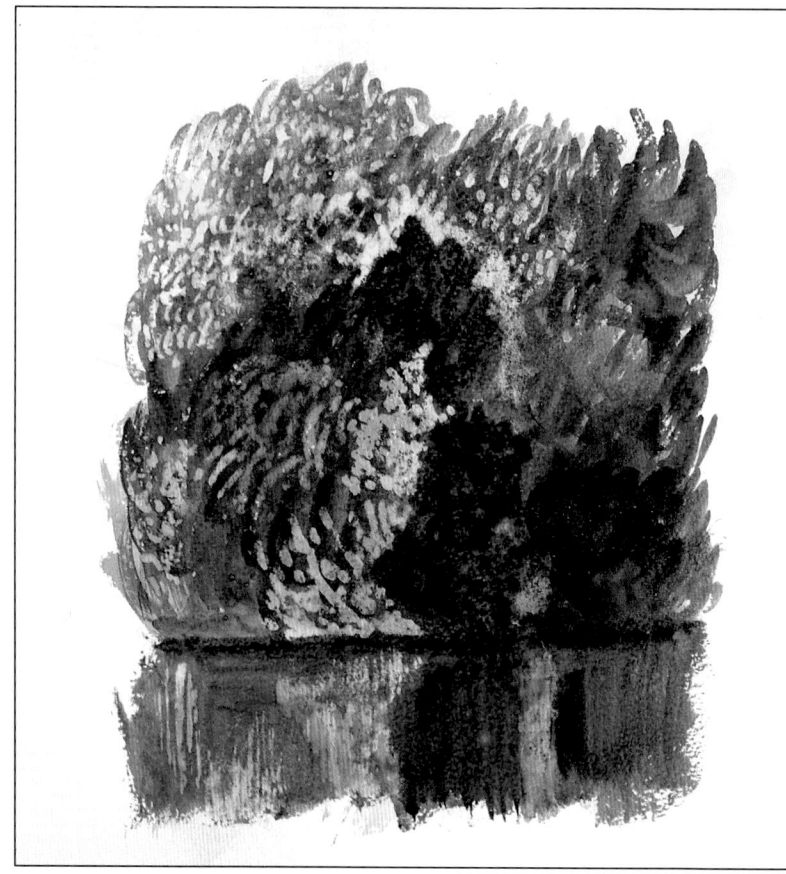

4 *(Left) You may find that gum water adds an extra dimension to your work; the effect of the lifted-out highlights is unlike anything achieved by standard methods. The artist herself, who had never used the technique before, was delighted.*

Mixing paint with soap

1 *The brush has been dipped into a strong solution of colour and rubbed over a bar of soap. This thickens the paint so that it holds the marks of the brush without sacrificing the transparency of the colour.*

2 *A bristle brush gives a different effect because the soapy paint can be used more thickly, in swirling strokes so that it forms ridges and bubbles. These remain when the paint has dried, creating an intriguing impression of specks and small circles.*

Watercolour and turpentine

1 *The brush has been dipped first into turpentine and then into paint, thus creating a striated effect as the paint withdraws from the oily substance of the turpentine.*

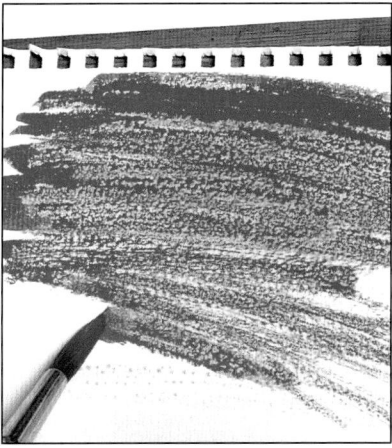

2 *Here turpentine has been scrubbed over the whole surface of the paper with a bristle brush before paint is applied on top.*

3 *The same method has been used for this example, but the brushstrokes are not as close together, having been drawn out to produce a light, scratchy texture.*

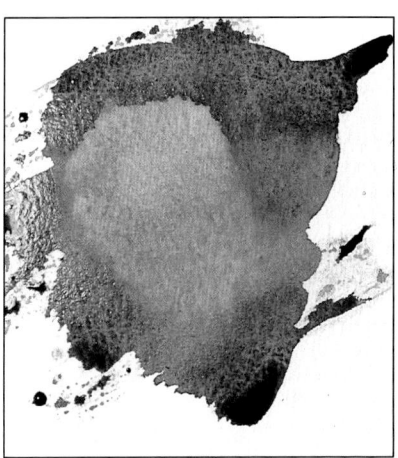

4 *In this case turpentine has been dropped into a wet wash; the water-and-paint mixture is then pushed outwards to form a pale shape.*

Ox gall, another medium sold specially for watercolour work, has the opposite effect. This makes the paint flow more freely and is therefore known as a "water-tension breaker".

So much for the conventional additives. There are some interesting "alternative" ones too, such as soap. This has a similar effect to gum arabic, thickening the paint so that it holds the marks of the brush, but with an added dimension – the bubbles, which form as you work, leave intriguing rings and blobs when dry. Soap is particularly useful for creating texture

effects and could be ideal for a dramatic stormy sky.

You can also create interesting effects in watercolour by exploiting a variation of the wax-resist technique. In this case turpentine is used which, being an oily substance, repels the watercolour. If you lay down some turpentine and then paint over it, the paint and the oil will separate, but only partially, giving a streaky or marbled appearance. Alternatively you can mix up some paint and dip your brush into turpentine before applying it. Like all such methods, this one is unpredictable but fun to try.

COMPARATIVE DEMONSTRATION

Non-professional watercolour painters sometimes restrict themselves unnecessarily by following, or studying under, one particular artist, trying to paint in exactly the same style. This can be valuable – artists have always been influenced by their teachers or by artists of the past whom they admire – but it can mislead you into thinking that there is only one way of doing things and that certain techniques are somehow wrong. To show that no two people work in the same way, we have asked two different artists to paint the same subject using their preferred method.

John Lidzey uses a combination of wet-into-wet and wet-on-dry methods, painting on smooth (hot-pressed) paper, because he likes to encourage the colours to run into each other and to form pools and backruns. Rosalind Cuthbert, on the other hand, paints on medium (Not surface) paper, using the classic wet-on-dry technique.

(Above) *An attractive still life of blue glass and silver objects is assembled on a checked tablecloth.*

Watercolour on smooth paper

1 *To make it easier to judge the colours needed for the silver bowl, the artist begins by laying light washes over the background. A careful pencil drawing was made first in order to keep these early washes away from the edges of the objects.*

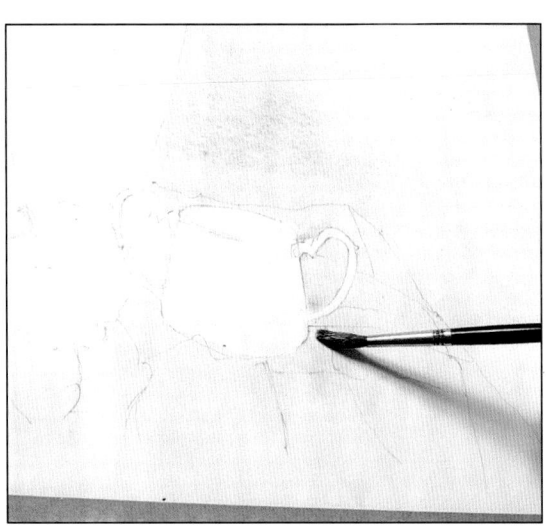

2 *For the main body of the vase, a soft effect has been created by painting wet into wet, but the white highlights must be sharply defined, so these have been reserved by painting carefully around them. Parts of this orange-yellow wash will in turn be reserved as highlights, together with the small patch on the right, which has been left white.*

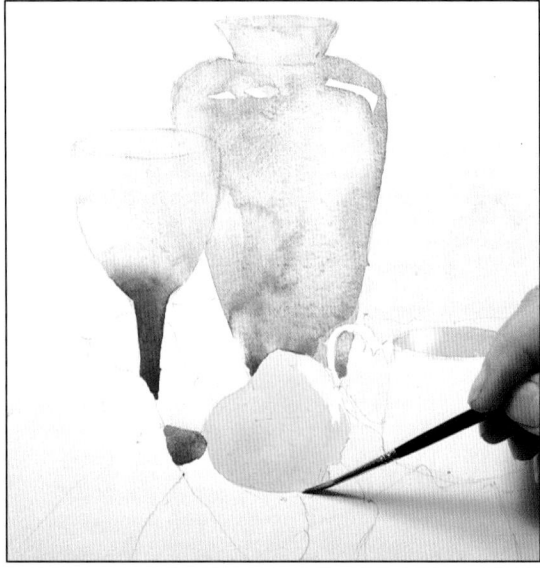

3 *The artist's method is to use wet-into-wet techniques only for certain areas of the painting; both here and on the silver pot he produces clean, clear edges by working wet on dry, drying the picture with a hairdryer between each stage.*

4 A darker wash laid on the apple is dabbed with cotton wool (a cotton ball) to create a softly diffused highlight. Cotton wool (cotton balls) and a hairdryer are both important items in the artist's "tool-kit".

5 The background colour is taken carefully around the edges of the glass. Although the glass and vase have been painted mainly wet into wet – you can see the effect clearly in this photograph – the painting has been dried to prevent the new colour from bleeding into the blue.

6 To soften areas of the background and provide a slight variation in tone and colour, damp cotton wool (a cotton ball) is again employed to lift out some of the wet paint. Granulation, one of the attractive accidental effects which watercolourists like to exploit, often occurs on smooth paper.

7 Here you can see how the original wash laid on the apple in Step 2 has been reserved for highlight effects, with the darker colours painted over it wet on dry. The added dark shadow gives the apple extra solidity.

8 The combination of soft, wet-into-wet effects and crisp, clean edges is very attractive. The treatment of the silver bowl and the top of the vase shows the importance of a preliminary drawing in watercolour work; each highlight and patch of reflected colour must be precisely placed, in order to explain the forms of the objects.

Continued ▷

Wet on dry on medium paper

1 *As in the previous demonstration, the artist has begun with an underdrawing, although here the lines are lighter. Unlike the other artist, she does not begin with the background, but establishes the colours of the glass and vase immediately.*

2 (Above) *As blue is the dominant colour in the painting, no other colours have yet been introduced. Two main blues have been used – ultramarine for the vase and Winsor (phthalocyanine) blue, a cooler, greener colour, for the glass and cloth.*

3 *The artist plans to key the background and foreground colours to those of the vase and bottle, therefore she concentrates on these first. The dark ultramarine now being used has also been laid over much of the glass, with some of the lighter blues reserved for highlights.*

4 (Right) *Light yellow washes are laid on the cloth and apple and, where the yellow is painted over the light blue, the two colours mix to produce green. A warmer, more orangey yellow has been painted over the blue at the bottom of the vase, which reflects colour from the apple.*

5 *By completing the vase before the other objects, the artist is able to evaluate the strength of the colours needed for the apple and its reflection in the silver bowl, which she paints next.*

6 (Right) *The broken colour of the apple and the inside of the silver bowl have been achieved by stippling, a version of the dry-brush technique, which is used once more for this shadow. Taking up the minimum of paint with the brush, the artist dabs it lightly onto the paper.*

9 In the final stages, a few further light washes were laid on the tablecloth to strengthen it slightly, and the area of background behind the table was darkened with a warm blue-grey. This is the one area of the painting in which colours were blended wet into wet, to achieve the required soft effect.

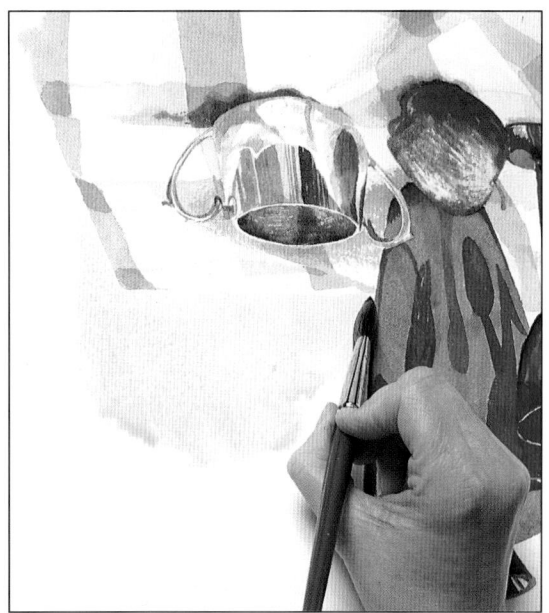

7 Leaving the background until last is often a good idea in still-life painting, as sometimes you do not know what kind of background is needed until the objects have been painted. Here a yellow similar to that of the cloth is chosen; the board is turned upside-down to facilitate the laying of the wash.

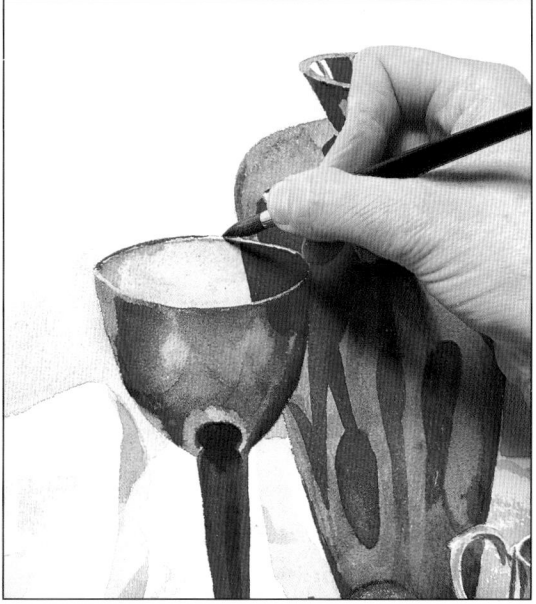

8 To give objects such as the blue glass extra definition and impact, fine highlights are added where edges catch the light.

LANDSCAPE

In most people's minds, watercolour is perhaps more closely associated with landscape than with any other subject. This may be because there is a long tradition of sketching in watercolour but, whatever the reason, there is no doubt that the fluidity and brilliance of watercolour, together with its portability, make it an excellent medium for on-the-spot painting.

Of course, you don't have to work directly from life all the time – we will be looking at alternative methods later on. If you are interested in landscape, however, it is advisable to do at least some location work, as there is no substitute for a direct response to your subject. Before you begin to translate your response into paint, you must make some initial decisions about how you are going to organize your picture in terms of composition.

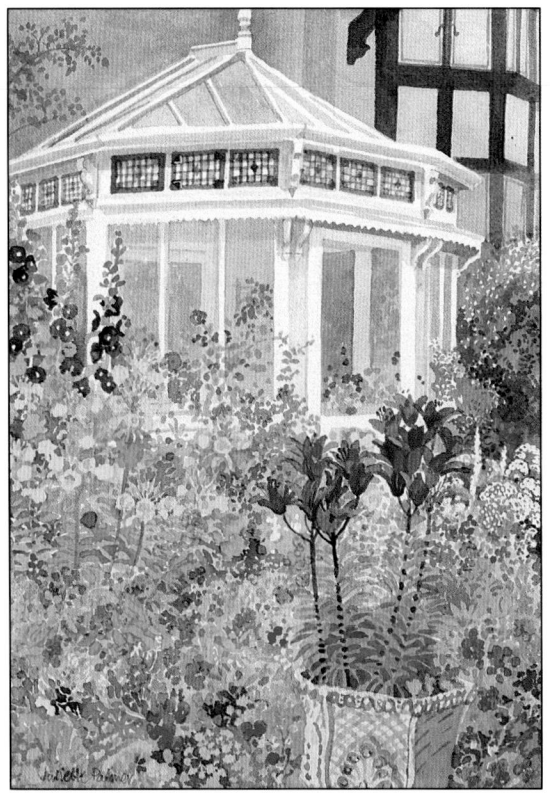

Unity and contrast
In the landscape shown below, Juliette Palmer has created visual links between the sky and the land areas by using similar shapes for both the small clouds and the trees. This has given an overall unity to her composition, with the straight lines of the houses providing contrast. In The Conservatory (left) *she has exploited this kind of contrast more thoroughly, using the geometric shapes and light colours of the architectural features as a foil for the free forms and bright colours of the flowers.*

Placing a focal point
(Left) *If there is one particular feature in your chosen view which catches your attention, such as a dark tree against a light background or a vivid area of colour, it will become the focal point in your painting, and you must decide where to place it and how to emphasize it. In Juliette Palmer's* Peak District – Springtime *the focal point (the white house) has been placed slightly off-centre, and the eye is led towards it by the curving diagonals of the foreground field and wall and the strong shape of the tall tree*

Making visual links

(Above) *Foregrounds are a frequent cause of failure in landscape composition; often they are treated in more detail than the middle distance and distance, making the picture look disconnected. In* From the Mule Path with Fig *Joan Elliott Bates has treated the foreground with the minimum of definition, but has taken care to link the fig tree to the rest of the picture both by letting the branches overlap the buildings and by using similar curving lines for the hills beyond.*

MAKING THE PICTURE

Even though you are simply painting what you can see, you still need to compose your picture. This doesn't mean that you have to move trees around or invent shadows where there are none, but you do have to decide what viewpoint to take, which part of the scene to concentrate on, how much of the picture you will devote to foreground and so on. Before you start, walk around a bit to find the position that gives you the most interesting angle on the subject; once you have chosen the viewpoint you are halfway to composing the picture.

However, you still need to decide where to place the horizon and to consider whether there are any elements in the scene which you can emphasize for effect, or any which you can play down or perhaps leave out altogether. You are not copying the

Creating movement

(Right) *A good landscape painting should encourage the viewer's eye to travel into and around the scene, to create movement in the composition. In* Road to Ronda *Pip Carpenter has achieved this quality both through her energetic brushwork and the way she has organized the picture. The area of trees and barely defined grass on the left leads towards the curving path, which the eye naturally follows. Paths, roads, streams or rivers leading from foreground to background are common compositional devices.*

scene; you are making your own statement about it and you don't have to include everything you see. After all, you would hardly try to paint every blade of grass in the foreground – you would generalize to create an impression of grass. So if there is a small, featureless shrub in the foreground which obscures your view of a grand tree further back, ignore it; alternatively, move your position so that it is less obtrusive.

The golden rule of composition is to avoid symmetry. It is never wise to divide your picture into halves, with the horizon exactly in the middle, particularly if it is a flat horizon line, as in a seascape. Nor should you place the most important element in the painting, for example a tree, right in the middle. Symmetry is dull and static and you should aim for a feeling of life and movement in your work.

KEEPING UP WITH THE LIGHT

Changing light is a constant problem for those who work out of doors. Even if the sun does not actually go in, thus removing all the shadows and much of the colour from the scene, it moves inexorably round the sky, altering the direction of the shadows and shining first on one side of a tree and then on the other.

The only way to cope with this is to work as fast as possible without actually rushing; restrict yourself to a fairly small scale so that you can cover the paper as quickly as possible. It is helpful to make a note of the direction of the light as soon as you begin. Either put a small pencil cross in a corner of the picture or block in the main shadows first – in this way, you won't be tempted to change them.

Do not try to work on the same painting over a whole day, unless it is overcast, because the scene you saw in the morning will be quite different from the one you see in the evening. It is better either to give yourself a definite time limit – say three hours – or to work on two consecutive days at the same time. Experienced painters can

Human interest
(Left) *You can often give additional interest to a landscape, or stress a centre of interest, by including one or two figures. In Ronald Jesty's* A Wild Day, *the men shielding their heads against the spray from the breaking wave and the woman pointing her hand in warning introduce an element of narrative, and both these and the surrounding dark rocks provide contrasts of tone which draw attention to the picture's focal point.*

often continue in the face of changing conditions, but only because they have well-trained visual memories and are sufficiently disciplined to stick to what they originally saw.

WORKING INDOORS

It is not really practical to paint big pictures out of doors, but a good method is to make a series of drawings and small colour sketches on location, then to compose and paint the actual picture indoors. This has the dual advantage of giving you direct experience of the subject and allowing you to paint at your own pace, incorporating any special techniques which you feel might improve the picture.

Making sketches for a painting, as opposed to simply sketching for the fun of it, is rather a special skill, as you must learn to give yourself sufficient visual information from which to work. Artists often make written notes about colours, shapes and so on in their sketchbooks, to help jog their memories when they are recreating a scene

later. Even when making colour sketches, try to back these up with suggestions to yourself – it is better to have too much information than too little.

You can also use photographs as a basis for painting. You may have been told that you should never work from photographs, but this is not realistic. Most painters have limited time at their disposal and the weather often makes outdoor work impossible, so it is better to paint from photographs than not to paint at all.

There are problems, however. The camera is seldom reliable over colour; it loses many subtle nuances and often reduces dark colours to a formless mass with no detail. Photographs also tend to flatten out perspective and reduce the feeling of three-dimensional space.

To give themselves a wider choice of possibilities, artists who use photographs usually take several versions of the subject, which they can then combine in their own composition. Sometimes they make sketches as well.

Studio paintings
(Above) *Patrick Cullen paints large-scale watercolours in the studio from sketches: this painting,* Landscape in La Crete Region, Tuscany, *is over five feet wide. Referring to sketches and drawings done on the spot, and sometimes making a working drawing to plan the composition, he paints area by area, building up deep, rich colours with a series of overlaid brushstrokes and occasionally washing down the paint to achieve soft gradations of tone and colour.*

DEMONSTRATION

Hazel Soan is known primarily as a watercolour landscape painter, although she does work in oils on occasion. She likes to paint on the spot whenever possible but, if time does not permit this, she composes her paintings in the studio, making extensive use of photographic reference. She seldom works from just one photograph, but uses a combination of several, selecting different elements from each and editing out unwanted features. The photographs are put away when she has reached a certain stage of work so that the painting can develop independently.

COLOURS

USED *mauve, permanent rose, cobalt blue, cerulean blue, ultramarine, yellow ochre, cadmium yellow, new gamboge, Winsor green, burnt sienna and a tiny amount of cadmium red*

1 The artist generally uses masking fluid to reserve highlight areas; here she begins to paint it in, referring to the photograph and guided by her initial light pencil drawing.

2 She builds up gradually from light washes to darker ones in the classic watercolour technique, working mainly wet on dry but using wet-into-wet methods in certain areas. A light rose pink and mauve mixture is laid over the masking fluid on the left of the picture to be rubbed into later on.

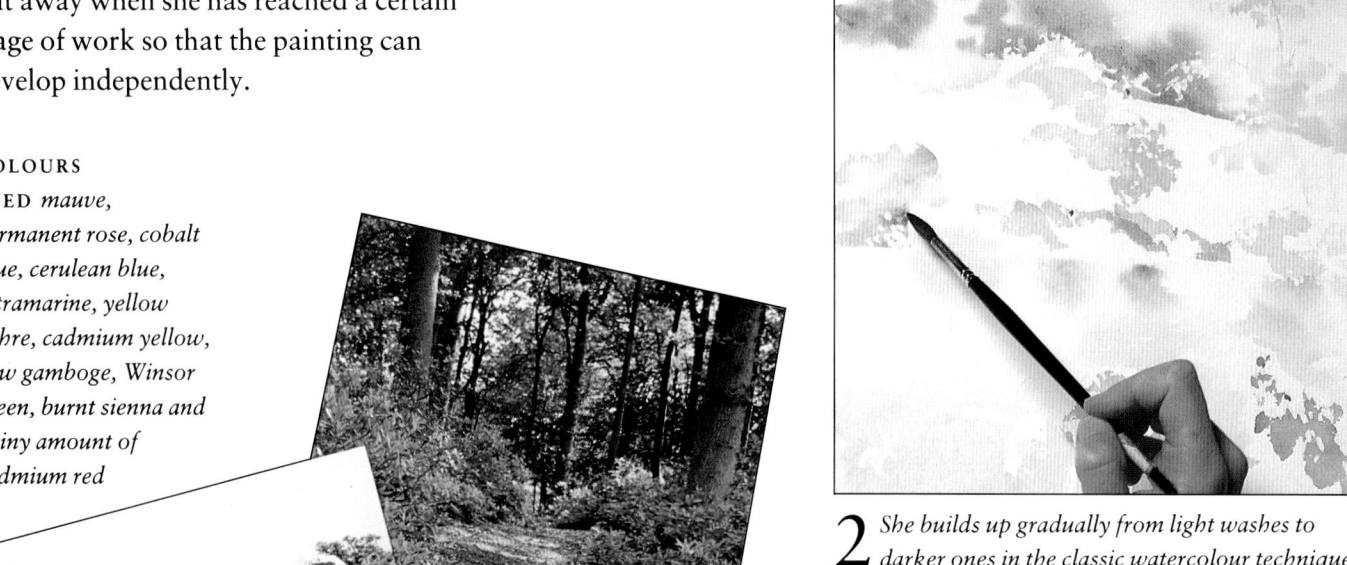

3 The colours of the flowers and the vivid red-brown of the foreground set the key for the overall warm colour scheme, so these are blocked in at an early stage.

5 *With the distant trees now complete, the artist turns her attention to the area on the far side of the lake. Here the colours are stronger but, for a relatively soft effect, the wet colours are blotted lightly so that they are not so saturated.*

4 *After about an hour's work, the main colours have been established, to be darkened and strengthened in places with further washes. The wet-into-wet method has so far been used only in the background, where soft effects are appropriate.*

6 *To strengthen the foreground, a dark mixture is painted over the light pink and red-brown washes. This area is worked wet on dry to achieve crisp edges, giving the foreground a sharper focus than the more distant parts of the landscape.*

7 *(Right) The masking fluid has been removed from some of the flowerheads, which are now touched in with pink. The fluid is removed at various stages during the painting, depending on how strong the highlights are to be.*

Continued ▷

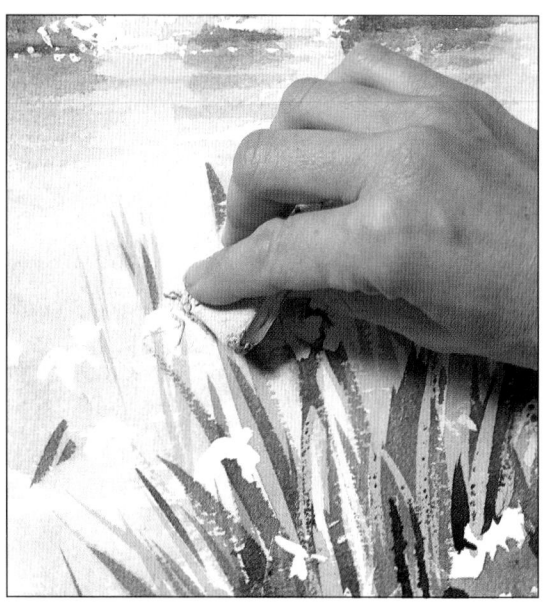

8 *The foliage of the large tree on the right had previously been painted wet into wet to give gentle blends of colour, with yellows merging into blue-greens. Crisp brushmarks now define those leaves nearer the foreground.*

9 *The masking fluid is removed from the flowerheads in the foreground by gently rubbing with a putty eraser. On the reeds it will be left in place, creating an attractive speckled texture similar to the effect of wax resist.*

10 *The flowers are now painted in yellow, with tiny patches of the white paper left uncovered. They could have been painted over the light blue of the water, without the use of masking fluid, but even the palest of underlying colours would have compromised the purity of this brilliant yellow.*

11 *Touches of deep pink are added to the flowerheads in the foreground of the picture.*

12 (Right) *In the final stages, the tonal contrasts in the foreground are strengthened to bring this area forward and increase the feeling of depth in the painting. The artist drops in dark colour wet into wet, using the tip of the brush.*

13 (Above) *The artist deliberated over whether to make more of the reflections, which were clearly visible in one of her photographs of the scene, but she decided against it, preferring to emphasize the triangular shape made by the pale expanse of water.*

FLOWERS

If landscape is the most popular subject for watercolour painters, flowers are not far behind. Sometimes, of course, the two subject areas overlap. When you are painting flowers in their natural habitat, perhaps in a garden or a park, you are painting a "mini-landscape", whereas flowers in a vase or bowl indoors become a floral still life.

Whether you paint flowers indoors or out (or both) is up to you, but for those who are new to flower painting it is perhaps best to avoid the problems of changing light, unreliable weather and discomfort. It demands concentration and patience to paint flowers. By setting up your own floral still life, you can take time to arrange it and then work at your own pace.

ARRANGING THE GROUP

Arranging any still-life group takes careful thought, and floral groups are no exception. First you must consider the balance of colours – in general you don't want too many different blooms, with all the shapes and colours fighting for attention. The most effective flower paintings are often those with one predominant colour. You could choose all white flowers, for example, or a selection of blue ones, perhaps with one yellow flower for contrast.

Choose a receptacle which suits the flowers, making them look neither cramped nor swamped. Aim for a natural look and avoid the kind of formal, official arrangement that you sometimes see in churches and public places. Let some of the flowers overlap; have some higher than others, some turned away and others facing you.

PUTTING IT ON PAPER

You will paint more confidently if you start with a good drawing, but, before you begin,

Keeping it simple

(Below) *The kind of elaborate groups beloved of florists do not always make the best paintings, so when you begin to arrange your flowers see if you can improve the composition by limiting their number. In Poppies Elisabeth Harden has given impact to the shapes and colours of the poppies by concentrating on a few flowerheads, including one or two small white flowers and seedheads for contrast. As the red against the dark green foliage in the foreground makes such a dramatic statement, she has wisely left the background unpainted.*

Flowers in still life

(Left) *Flowers do not have to be painted on their own; they can form part of a more general still life, as in* Still Life, Welsh Kitchen *by Joan Elliott Bates. The flowers are the main centre of interest, but the objects and curtain have been carefully arranged, as they play a subsidiary but vitally important role in the composition. Notice particularly the way the curtain sweeps around and upwards, creating a strong curve which provides a foil for the flowers and vase. This is a mixed-media painting, in which watercolour has been combined with Conté crayon and pastel.*

consider how to place the group of flowers on your paper. Again, try to avoid symmetry; don't place the vase exactly in the middle of the picture unless there is enough asymmetry in the arrangement itself to balance this. Decide how much of the group you are going to include. A device often used is "cropping", which means allowing one or two blooms and stems to go out of the picture at the top. This can be very effective if you are painting tall flowers, while a wider group could be cropped at one side or the other.

The foreground and background need consideration too. Avoid leaving a blank space on either side of the vase. Sometimes

this can be done by making a positive element out of the shadow cast by the vase; other alternatives are to put the vase on a patterned cloth or to take out one or two of the flowers and place them in front, to one side of the vase.

Backgrounds in watercolour flower painting are often left vague and undefined, but they don't have to be. If there is a window behind the group you could lightly suggest it, thus giving a geometric framework to the composition. Or you could set the group against a patterned wallpaper, which might echo and reinforce the pattern made by the flowers themselves. As a general rule, however, it is best to

Colour unity

(Above) *In* Daffodils and Fruit *Elisabeth Harden has paid attention to the colour schemes, ensuring that links are established between the flowers and objects. The lemon and grapefruit echo the yellows of the daffodils, and similar blues and greys appear in the vase, cup and saucer, and tablecloth. The muted greens of the leaves give greater prominence to the whites, yellows and greys.*

Making a pattern
(Left) *There is a strong built-in pattern element in floral subjects, which has been exploited to the full in Audrey Macleod's Casablanca Lilies. Although the forms of the flowers and leaves have been built up carefully so that they are completely realistic and three-dimensional, the painting makes its initial impact as a pattern of light on dark. The soft effects on the leaves and in parts of the background were achieved by washing down the paint.*

avoid too much detail in the background or foreground – the flowers are the centre of interest in the painting, and, by introducing too many other elements, you could rob them of their importance.

THE PAINTING

The essence of flower painting is lightness of touch; if you overwork the paint the freshness of the colours will be lost. Try to work broadly and freely, at least initially, blocking in the main shapes and colours and reserving detail for the final stages. Masking fluid can help you here. If you are painting white or light-coloured flowers against a mass of green foliage, you can mask the flowers and leave them until a later stage in the painting.

Try to set up contrasts between hard and soft edges, using the wet-into-wet technique in some places and painting wet on dry in others to form crisper areas (perhaps for certain well-defined petals or leaves). Don't be tempted to put in small details until you are sure that all the shapes and colours are working as they should – only in the final stages should you bring your tiny, fine brush into play.

Single blooms

(Above) *Although flowers are more generally painted as an arrangement in a vase, individual flowers make equally rewarding subjects. The artists of China and Japan brought flower painting of this kind to a high art, and Vicky Lowe's lovely* Sunflower *owes much to the Oriental tradition, both in the composition and in the technique, with each petal described by one swift, sure brushstroke. The soft effect where the dark centre of the flower merges into the petals has been achieved by dampening selected areas and dropping in wet paint.*

Using colour
(Opposite) *The way you treat flowers, or any other subject, depends on what it is that particularly interests you. For Gerry Baptist, colour is all-important; in* Clandon Garden Flowers *he has made the most of the brilliant reds and yellows by contrasting them with cool blues, mauves and dark greens. He has also paid attention to the flower shapes, however, and the pansies in the foreground in particular are clearly recognizable.*

Foregrounds and backgrounds

(Right) *When painting a tall floral group it can be difficult to know what to do with the area below and beside the vase. In Elisabeth Harden's painting of poppies, Audrey Macleod's* Casablanca Lilies *and this watercolour-and-wax-resist painting,* Roses, *by Debra Manifold, the artists have solved the problem by cropping the vase at the bottom of the picture. Here, the way in which the flowers merge into the dark background is also important to the composition, with the dark shape seeming to push upwards away from the pale foreground area, almost like a firework exploding.*

DEMONSTRATION

John Lidzey works entirely in watercolour, enjoying the challenge of its unpredictable nature and the way it encourages the painting to develop in its own way. He paints mainly landscapes and lovely light-filled interiors, the latter often including still lifes and flower groups. He is self-taught and has evolved a highly personal style, at which he arrived through experiment rather than the study of any other artist's methods. He enjoys wet-into-wet effects, although he controls them carefully, and usually paints on smooth-surfaced (hot-pressed) paper to allow the paint to move around more freely.

COLOURS USED *yellow ochre, aureolin yellow, cadmium yellow, ultramarine, cadmium red, carmine, indigo, Payne's gray*

(Above) To start with, the artist arranges some bright, contrasting flowers in a vase.

1 *The artist begins with a detailed drawing in 4B pencil. He takes considerable care with this, measuring to check the relative proportions of flowers to vase and so on, and making small marks across the paper to establish key points.*

2 *The vase and the shadow beneath are painted wet into wet, with one colour dropped into another so that they merge and mingle. A piece of cotton wool (a cotton ball) is used to control the flow of the paint.*

3 *The initial applications of paint are allowed to dry slightly; darker colour is then painted on top and dabbed with cotton wool (a cotton ball) to create soft highlights.*

4 *It is unusual to begin with the darkest colour – darks are generally built up gradually. In this case, however, the artist wanted to establish the deep blue of the vase in order to assess the strength of colour needed for the leaves.*

5 *The painting is at approximately the halfway stage, with the darkest colours in place and the white flowers reserved as bare paper.*

6 *A good deal of the paper is to be left uncovered for the flowers, but they must be given sufficient detail to suggest their structure. A fine-pointed brush is used to touch in the blue-grey shadow.*

7 *Carnations have a very distinctive petal formation; only a few touches of darker paint over the original pink wash are needed to describe their forms and character. The artist is working wet on dry here, to achieve the necessary crisp edges and strong tonal contrasts.*

8 *(Above) Finally, the flowers and leaves are built up with further wet-on-dry work. The pencil marks on the white flowers have been deliberately left showing, to provide further suggestions of detail. The artist subsequently improves the composition by placing paper masks at top and bottom to cut down the rather featureless expanses of foreground and background; look back at Step 5 to see what a difference this makes.*

INDEX

PUBLISHER'S
ACKNOWLEDGEMENTS

The Author and Publisher would like to thank the following companies for supplying materials used in the making of this book.

Cornelissen & Son Ltd
105 Great Russell Street
London WC1B 3RY

Daler-Rowney Ltd
PO Box 10
Southern Industrial Estate
Bracknell
Berkshire
RG12 8ST

Russell & Chapple Ltd
Canvas & Art Materials
23 Monmouth Street
London WC2H 9DE

Winsor & Newton
Whitefriars Avenue
Wealdstone
Harrow
Middlesex
HA3 5RH